Eerie Britain
&
Eerie Britain 2

Twenty of Britain's Most Terrifying and
Peculiar Real-Life Stories

By MB Forde

Eerie Britain
&
Eerie Britain 2
Twenty of Britain's Most Terrifying and Peculiar Real-Life
Stories
by MB Forde.
First published July 2013.

ISBN: 1483994538
ISBN-13: 978-1483994536

AUTHOR'S NOTE

Thank you for buying this combined, print edition of the ebooks *Eerie Britain* and *Eerie Britain 2*. Instead of merging the two into a larger volume they are presented to you here in their original forms, back to back. Happy reading.

Eerie Britain

Ten of Britain's Most Terrifying and
Peculiar Real-Life Stories

By MB Forde

Eerie Britain
Ten of Britain's Most Terrifying and Peculiar Real-Life Stories
by MB Forde.
First published December 2011.

Ebook edition's ASIN: B006J5LVJY

For Katy

Eerie Britain

CONTENTS

A BRISK PREFACE

With ancient ruins, handsome countryside and quaint customs, Britain is a pleasant spot. Furthermore, (and, perhaps most importantly,) roast dinners, hearty puddings and steaming pots of tea abound. But lo, the heart-warming features of British life aren't the only things to be found upon this venerable archipelago, for it seems that around every corner there lurks a ferocious monster legend, a mysterious tale or a terrifying phantom—ready to jump out and scare the pants off you.

Perfectly good farmhouses harbour mischievous poltergeists and snowy mountain ranges are home to baffling spectres, while foreboding castles and country houses list royal apparitions among their denizens. This then, is a land with more ghost stories than you can shake an EMF detector at.

Of course, whether ghouls and goblins actually exist is a topic that is endlessly debated by many, and no doubt it shall remain that way for decades—if not centuries—to come. Some people say that apparitions and the like are merely figments of the complex human mind, others that they are a type of mysterious recording that is somehow imprinted upon places and buildings. Then, there are also those who insist spectres and suchlike are actually the spirits of the restless dead, returned to walk upon the Earth. Whatever the truth may be and whatever you believe yourself, there is no denying that many of the stories that surround hauntings are rich and fascinating tales. Indeed, in this regard it hardly matters whether the ghosts, monsters and poltergeists that feature are genuinely otherworldly or entirely made up. With that in mind, we shall concentrate here upon the anecdotal riches that these grisly tales offer us and less upon the more technical aspects of ghost hunting that have become popular in recent years.

Many of these weird and wonderful stories are

hundreds of years old, with origins that have long been lost amid the swirling fog of time, and it is often difficult (if not impossible) to tell which author or legend gives the most accurate or authoritative account. Where numerous versions of the same story exist I have endeavoured to make mention of the most important and relevant aspects of all of them, and, of course, have corroborated points where possible.

In the final pages there lies a recommended reading section. The entries there offer more details, alternative versions of the stories and cases included in this publication, or they simply make for excellent reads for those of you who would like to further your knowledge.

And so, herein lurks a selection of Britain's most strange, terrifying and peculiar stories. So pull your blanket tightly around your shoulders, ignite your pipe and take warmth from the steaming mug of hot chocolate next to you as our journey into the macabre begins...

From ghoulies and ghosties and long-leggedy beasties,
And things that go bump in the night,
Good Lord, deliver us!

Eerie Britain

1

Am Fear Liath Mhor: The Terrifying Grey Man of the Cairngorms

Does an ethereal giant stalk the slopes of one of Britain's highest peaks?

In the eastern highlands of Scotland, on the boundary between Aberdeenshire and Moray, there exists one of the wildest and most remote places in the British Isles. Here, where only the hardiest of mountain flora grow, is an epic landscape that is at the same time harsh, humbling and achingly beautiful. For this is the Cairngorms mountain range (Am Monadh Ruadh); an ancient place that has long compelled the adventurous to seek out its snowy slopes. And it is Ben MacDhui, with a height of 4,296 feet (1,309 metres) that stands as the range's highest peak. But, it's not just the forces of nature that mountaineers have to contend with here, for it is said that a terrifying and evil figure stalks the wind-whipped backdrop of Ben MacDhui, seeking out climbers and sending them fleeing from the mountain in alarm.

Locals call this 'Am Fear Liath Mhor', but beyond these lands it is more widely known by its English name: 'The Big Grey Man'. Sightings are uncommon, but there have been enough to suggest that this phenomenon is something more than just the made-up stories of bored hikers. Indeed, tales of encounters with this entity have been related by visitors to the peaks since the 1700s.

Reports differ little in describing the figure, with most agreeing that the Big Grey Man, or the 'Greyman' as it is sometimes known, is just that—a very tall, grey figure. How it manifests itself is far more varied, though: sometimes it looms suddenly from out of the mountain mist, while on other occasions it affects climbers as waves of strong emotions that overcome them. It can even reveal itself as eerie, disembodied footsteps that crunch in the snow alongside horrified climbers.

The first report of this enigmatic entity to reach a wide audience came from renowned mountaineer and Fellow of the Royal Society, Professor John Norman Collie of University College London. Collie surprised the attendees of the 1925 annual general meeting of the Cairngorm Club by giving a speech that described an experience he'd had on the mountain in 1891. What he said has now become a very well-known account and is oft-quoted in articles about the Big Grey Man. Not wanting to be left out, I include it here:

> "I was returning from the cairn on the summit in a mist when I began to think I heard something else than merely the noise of my own footsteps. Every few steps I took, I heard a crunch and then another crunch, as if someone was walking after me but taking steps three or four times the length of my own. I said to myself, this is all nonsense. I listened and heard it again but could see nothing in the mist.
>
> "As I walked on and the eerie crunch, crunch sounded behind me I was seized with terror and took to my heels, staggering blindly among the boulders for four or five

miles nearly down to Rothiemurchus forest.
Whatever you make of it I do not know, but
there is something very queer about the top
of Ben MacDui and I will not go back there
again myself, I know."

Collie's reputation as a highly experienced mountaineer
and a man of credibility (he had no less than two peaks
named after him: one on the Isle of Skye and another in
Canada) made people sit up and listen, and after his
account circulated it prompted more witnesses to come
forward with tales of their own encounters.

In 1904, Hugh Welsh and his brother had set up their
camp near the summit of Ben MacDhui to collect plants
and study the wildlife found there. From time-to-time they
would hear what sounded like footsteps impacting softly
around them whenever they moved. These footsteps did
not match their own footfalls and the brothers noted that
the curious sounds were more distinct during the daylight
hours. The brothers added that while this was going on
they were "very conscious of 'something' near them".

Thirty-seven years later, the eccentric Scottish
Nationalist, Wendy Wood (born Gwendoline Meacham),
was advancing upon the well-known hill pass of Lairig
Ghru when a strange voice, speaking in what sounded like
Gaelic, reached her, carried upon the winter air. Wood
later said the voice had "gigantic resonance". Despite a
brief search, Wood found no source for the voice, but her
encounter was not quite over, for as she made her way
back, she began to hear the same footsteps that the Welsh
brothers had heard—and they seemed to be following her.
At first she thought the sounds to simply be echoes of her
own steps, but it rapidly became clear that they did not
match their rhythm and, frightened, she promptly fled.

It was these phantom footsteps that also startled the
leader of the Cairngorms RAF Rescue Team during the
Second World War. Peter Densham, another person who
knew the area well, reported feeling "overwhelmed with

panic" after hearing the footfalls around him while within a heavy mist. Like so many others, he left the mountain in haste, scrambling perilously close to a cliff's edge and feeling as though something intangible was trying to send him over it: "I tried to stop myself and found this extremely difficult to do. It was as if someone was pushing me. I managed to deflect my course, but with a great deal of difficulty."

And the footsteps are not alone in spooking some of Ben MacDhui's climbers. Visitors have experienced a baffling whining or ringing noise, sudden feelings of terror or engulfing despondency, while others, like Peter Densham, have felt "hypnotically drawn to the edges of cliffs".

But, it is not just the intangible nature of the Big Grey Man that people have witnessed, for sometimes the entity reveals itself entirely—and when it does, it is not for the faint-hearted.

In the early 1920s, former president of the Moray Mountaineering Club, Tom Crowley, heard the footsteps as he was descending Braeriach (a peak to the west of Ben MacDhui's, across the Lairig Ghru pass) into Glen Eanaich. He paused and turned his head to cast a glance over his shoulder and was alarmed to see a tall figure, grey, undefined and with "pointed ears, long legs and finger-like talons on its feet" approaching him from behind.

Alexander Mitchell Kellas was another very experienced climber and, like John Norman Collie, a man of science. Together with his brother Henry, Kellas was close to the mountain's summit when they spotted a "giant figure" moving towards them from the direction of the Lairig Ghru pass. The Scottish chemist watched the shape walk to the summit, circle the ten-foot-tall cairn there (the figure matched the cairn's height) and then disappear back into the pass from whence it came.

The author of *The Big Grey Man of Ben MacDhui*, Richard Frere, outlined a tale that had been related to him by a friend. This friend had established his camp at the very top of the mountain sometime in 1940. As darkness fell, the man retreated into his tent to settle down for the evening. A little while later, he awoke suddenly and noticed movement outside his tent's opening. Something strange was close by, and as he peered out of his tent into the night there loomed a large, broad-shouldered and "brownish" humanoid creature that must have been twenty feet in height. It seemed to swagger as it moved around the camp, emitting an "air of insolent strength" before it eventually moved off by itself. Yet another climber, the legendary William Sydney Scroggie, saw a similar humanoid figure emerge from out of darkness in 1942 before disappearing.

One man actually shot at the Big Grey Man. In 1943, Alexander Tewnion was climbing by himself on the mountain, in search of some game. It was the month of October, and a chilly mist descended around him as he walked along the wild Coire Etchachan. Without warning, a massive figure appeared out of the swirling mist in front of him. Naturally, Tewnion's thoughts went to the revolver he was carrying and he reached for it and aimed it at the thing ahead of him. He fired off all the gun's chambers at close range but saw that his attack had no effect. Tewnion ran for it, reaching Glen Derry in what he said was his personal best time. His account appeared in *The Scots Magazine* in June 1958:

> "I am not unduly imaginative, but my thought flew instantly to the well known story of Professor Collie and the Fear Liath Mhor. Then I felt the reassuring weight of the loaded revolver in my pocket. Grasping the butt, I peered about in the mist here rent and tattered by the eddies of wind. A strange shape loomed up, receded, came charging at me! Without hesitation I whipped out the revolver and fired three times at the figure. When it still came on I turned and hared

down the path, reaching Glen Derry in a time that I have never bettered.

"You may ask was it really the Fear Laith Mhor? Frankly, I think it was. Many times since then I have traversed MacDhui in the mist, bivouacked out in the open, camped on its summit for days on end on different occasions—often alone and always with an easy mind. For, on that day I am convinced I shot the only Fear Liath Mhor my imagination will ever see."

Explanations for what the Big Grey Man of Ben MacDhui might be vary greatly. Some say it is a kind of spectral sentinel, guarding an 'inter-dimensional gateway' of some kind. Others have placed mystical ley 'lines' at the heart of the strange goings-on. Some people simply believe that ten-foot-tall grey creatures might actually exist in the form of a cryptid, rather like the elusive Yeti or Bigfoot, and that there is nothing supernatural about the Big Grey Man at all, merely that it is an extremely rare and elusive animal that is as yet undiscovered by science.

More down-to-earth speculation centres upon the meteorological phenomenon known as the 'Brocken spectre', a rare event during which a spectator can see their own elongated shadow cast against clouds, mist or fog, sometimes accompanied by a rainbow-like halo known as a 'glorie'. While the Brocken spectre theory goes some way to explaining the long-legged, tall, grey figures that have been sighted, it doesn't tackle the other aspects of the reports, such as the weird, disembodied footsteps and the strange emotions.

Perchance oxygen starvation is to blame, as some have pointed out. The effects of high altitudes and the ease of becoming disoriented amongst the Cairngorms' featureless and flat-topped peaks could combine to produce light-headedness and panic and so distort a person's rationality. But, perhaps the most fascinating aspect to the sightings of the Big Grey Man is that they so often come from sources that would be considered eminently reliable and level-headed, otherwise. These are individuals that are experienced mountaineers—people who may well have been familiar with phenomena like the Brocken Spectre and certainly knew about the effects of thin air at high heights and yet not only did they claim to see a supernatural creature, but they fled in terror at it and admitted doing so to a public audience, risking ridicule.

Whatever stalks Ben MacDhui is unlikely to be classified soon, but what is certain is that the Cairngorms are a primeval and commanding location where nature's majesty is more than apparent, and in landscapes such as these, it is almost necessary that, if no great legend were associated with it, one would have to be invented.

2

The MacKenzie Poltergeist

*A terrible and well-documented evil lurks within this infamous
Edinburgh mausoleum.*

In December of 1998, a homeless man wandered through
Edinburgh's storm-lashed streets. Seeking shelter from the
night's downpour he staggered into Greyfriars Kirkyard
and broke into one of the old mausoleums in the
Covenanter's Prison section—no doubt attracted by its
intact roof. Inside, the vault was pitch-black and the brave
(or foolhardy) vagrant decided to explore his surroundings
with what meagre light he possessed. He removed an iron
grate in the floor and descended a short, twisting, stone
staircase and entered a second chamber. There, he came
across four wooden coffins. Perhaps looking for valuables
to steal, the man began to smash open the dusty caskets.
As he did so, a hole suddenly opened beneath his feet and
he fell through a wooden division into a third chamber—
the existence of which had been previously unknown. The
unfortunate intruder landed in a deep pit that had been
used for illegally dumping those that had died from the
plague. Despite being hundreds of years old, the pit had
remained well-sealed and the corpses that greeted the

luckless tramp were far from skeletal. Semi-putrefied and covered in green slime, the rotten carcasses had sunken features, ragged clothing, matted hair and emitted an overpowering stench.

Not surprisingly, the man desperately fled the tomb, not stopping even when he cut his head on the tomb's entrance in his reckless flight.

A nearby security guard and his dog had heard strange noises coming from the Covenanter's Prison and were in the process of exploring the graveyard when they saw the wailing vagrant hurtling towards them. The sight of a bloody, filthy and bedraggled man charging out of a crypt in the middle of a stormy night was too much for the guard and both men fled separately into Edinburgh's darkness.

The security guard turned up for work the next day, related the tale of his terrifying encounter and promptly handed in his notice. The tramp, however, was never heard from again.

And frankly, he couldn't have chosen a more sinister vault to break into, for its name is the Black Mausoleum and to this day it houses the remains of the most notorious resident of Greyfriars Kirkyard: the 17th century judge and Lord Advocate Sir George MacKenzie, otherwise known to the Scots as "Bluidy MacKenzie". Made Advocate in August 1677 by King Charles II, MacKenzie organised an enthusiastic and bloody prosecution of Covenanters in retaliation for their refusal to replace Scotland's Presbyterian Church with the Episcopalian Church that had come to dominate England to the south.

The summer of 1679 saw defeat for the Covenanters at the Battle of Bothwell Bridge and 3,000 of them were captured. MacKenzie brought them to Greyfriars where some were hanged and some beheaded, their rotting skulls displayed on walls around the city. Others were tortured publicly while a thousand were dispersed among other prisons or allowed to go free.

The remainder were kept corralled at a section of land

adjacent to Greyfriars Kirkyard in a makeshift, open air prison that would become the first recorded concentration camp. By mid-November of that year, most of the 1,200 ill-fated detainees had died from starvation, disease or exposure to the harsh Scottish winter. The surviving few hundred were packed onto a ship bound for Australia. It is estimated that MacKenzie was responsible for the deaths of 18,000 unfortunate Covenanters, his own countrymen, during a reign of terror now referred to as 'The Killing Time'.

An infamously brutal man, indeed.

In seeking a place to sleep for the night, the homeless man seems to have inadvertently awakened far more than he could have expected, for mysterious and disturbing activity was to be reported almost immediately after his unwitting interference with the mausoleum's contents. The very next day, an unnamed woman, peering through the iron grate set into the vault's door, was reportedly "blasted back off its steps by a cold force". Soon after, another female was discovered sprawled on the ground near the tomb, her neck ringed with heavy bruising. She claimed "that invisible hands had tried to strangle her". Similar injuries were found on another victim, this time a young man who was found lying opposite the vault.

Soon, it all became too much for Edinburgh City Council. They locked the Black Mausoleum's door and declared the location to be out of bounds to all but those with express permission to enter. That was until local author Jan-Andrew Henderson asked the council for permission to bring controlled tours to the mausoleum. The council acceded and now the City of the Dead Tour enjoys almost exclusive access to the menacing site, running regular visits. Since then, it seems that the paranormal activity has escalated alarmingly.

Phenomena at the Black Mausoleum stands out against that experienced at many other purportedly haunted locations in that it has been startlingly frequent in occurrence, often severe and very well-documented. Since

1998 there have been over 450 attacks—and that's just the reported incidents, who knows how high the number actually is? Amongst the 450, some 180 people have lost consciousness, inexplicable fires have broken out, weird cold spots abound and an unusually high number of dead wildlife has been found in the vault's immediate vicinity. People have had their fingers broken, hair pulled and felt as though something has punched or kicked them. Unexplained bruises, scratches and burns, skin gouges, nausea and numbness have all been frequently reported. Cameras and other electrical equipment malfunction in the area of the Mausoleum.

Intriguingly, the physical signs of attack often go unnoticed until people get home and relax or return to their hotels for the night. Only then do the unexplained injuries manifest. Some of the scratches and burns disappear as quickly as they emerge while others may last for months. Some though, scar for life. Furthermore, many of the frightening experiences don't end when the tour finishes. People have reported that some of the phenomena listed above actually *followed them home*, witnessing strange occurrences such as light bulbs blowing and electrical appliances switching on and off by themselves. One man, an ex-police officer who prefers to remain anonymous, described his experience to staff at the City of the Dead Tour:

> "After the tour I decided to go back to our hotel room. I was glancing at *'The Ghost that Haunted Itself'* [a book about the story of the Mackenzie Poltergeist by Jan-Andrew Henderson], when I felt a sharp burning sensation on the right hand side of my neck. There were at least five deep scrapes [that appeared just under my Adam's apple]. On returning home the next morning I went straight to my mother's house and told her my tale, along with handing her *The Ghost that*

Haunted Itself, which I had decided I did not want in my home. Yesterday I phoned her and asked her what she thought of the book. Remarkably, she was just examining five large scratches under her Adam's apple [that were] identical to my own. I am not the sort of individual who frightens easily but, hand on heart, I am very frightened now. The phenomenon you have in that graveyard prison is very real."

Sometimes, every participant of a particular tour will feel or see the same phenomena and so some of these events boast corroborative witnesses by the bucket load. Not only that, but Black Hart Entertainment, the company that runs the tours, keeps detailed records and photographs of the injuries sustained by visitors to the mausoleum and its surrounding area.

And the frightening events are not limited to physical attacks, either; the baffling aroma of smelling salts and the powerful stench of sulphur have been reported on occasion, while inexplicable laughing and growling has been heard along with strange knocking sounds that seem to emanate from beneath ground level. One tour member reported:

"We had not been in the Black Mausoleum long when we started hearing knocking noises coming from beneath us, which steadily grew louder and seemed to move up and round the walls..."

Interestingly, exorcisms have been carried out twice at the location, first by a spiritualist minister named Colin Grant and a year later by his son. Both were unsuccessful and the attacks continue. Jan-Andrew Henderson himself says:

"I am a very scientific person, and I don't know if I believe in ghosts or not, but I just don't have an explanation for the sheer number of people who have collapsed, had their fingers broken or whatever. I've even had phone calls from two people who say their partner has now been committed, and blame it on the ghost."

Seemingly, the poltergeist activity is not limited to the mausoleum. Smashed plates, unexplained fires and object aportation have been reported by the residents in four different houses that border the graveyard. Then, in October 2003, a large fire swept through both Jan-Andrew Henderson's nearby home and the Black Hart Entertainment offices. Henderson says that the fire—the cause of which insurance investigators could not identify—destroyed "five years worth of letters, photographs, records and statements concerning the MacKenzie Poltergeist as well as every possession I had in the world. None of the surrounding properties were damaged."

This apparently wide-roaming poltergeist is also thought by some to be the cause of a number of the malignant and odd activity in another of Edinburgh's infamously haunted locations: the South Bridge Vaults, although others argue against this notion with equal vigour.

Explanations for the spooky goings-on abound. Even before the bodies of the Covenanters were added to its earth, Greyfriars was a graveyard literally bursting with death and decay. Much larger than today's plot, it was established in 1562 and, topographically, was formerly a depression that sank twenty feet or more until, thanks to the combined effects of some 500,000 recorded burials, it became rather more of a hill, rising fifteen feet. Such is the concentration of human remains that on especially rainy days some of the bones of the long-since interred actually rise to the surface. It is said that it is not uncommon to spot the white gleam of a femur's end among the Kirkyard grass. So, the entire location, it seems, is a canvas perfectly primed for things that go bump in the night—surely if ghosts really do exist this would be one of the most fertile fields for them to spring forth from. Indeed, there have been many sightings of unidentifiable shapes lurking between the headstones: pallid figures, spectral white birds and wraithlike children.

But, in spite of the area's bloody history providing innumerable candidates for a ghostly perpetrator of the happenings at MacKenzie's tomb, hauntings are rarely this consistent or active. What's more, the kinds of attacks witnessed are far more redolent of a poltergeist. But this presents us with a problem too, as typically, poltergeist phenomena centre on an 'agent' who, often unknowingly, serves as a focus for the associated disturbances. No one living person could act as such a hub at the mausoleum. Also, research by Alan Gauld and A. D. Cornell established that barely a quarter of poltergeist episodes last more than a year, whereas whatever lurks within MacKenzie's tomb has been scaring people for over a decade now.

Another explanation, and one which Henderson and his tour guides often espouse, concerns pheromones. Pheromones are chemicals which are excreted or secreted and can influence the behaviour of other species members, most notably in insects. Humans can also be affected by these chemical signals. In the case of the Black Mausoleum it is hypothesised that the pheromones released by the intense emotions of those who were tortured, imprisoned and killed in the Covenanter's Prison have somehow been 'imprinted' upon the location and, combined with the fear and apprehension felt by modern-day visitors, it is this that is psychosomatically causing the nausea, coldness, dizziness and perhaps even the poltergeistesque activity. Indeed, some paranormal researchers think that poltergeists can actually move along pheromone trails, with the two being linked. If this is true it would go some way towards explaining why many of the tour members have reported the impression of being followed home from the Kirkyard by something sinister.

Of course, it is possible that the answer lies within environmental factors. To the rear of the Mausoleum is Edinburgh University's Artificial Intelligence Unit where high voltage machinery is housed. These machines can give off electromagnetic energy, a force that some believe could create hallucinations in people that are 'EM sensitive' and so be the explanation for certain paranormal activity. This again, however, does not explain the physical attacks that visitors to the vault have suffered.

A further environmental theory suggests that the answer might lie deep below ground; deeper even than Greyfriars' interred dead. According to the British Geological Survey at Murchison House in Edinburgh, sandstone forms much of the rock underneath the Greyfriars area. Brian Allan of Strange Phenomena Investigations suggests that saturated sandstone might be to blame. He argues that sandstone, when permeated with mineral electrolytes, could store energy which might be released under certain conditions and affect some peoples' temporal lobes.

As is often the case with hauntings that are said to have their roots in times long passed, there are many legends associated with MacKenzie's tomb. One of the more popular tales describes a failed petty criminal—possibly a highwayman—named John Hayes who, fleeing justice and the police, found shelter in the second chamber of the Black Mausoleum.

For six long months Hayes secreted himself within the vault, scavenging food wherever he could. Eventually, when the local police caught up with him, they found him to be completely insane, insisting that the coffins that kept him company would move each night of their own accord and that 'Bluidy MacKenzie' could be heard shuffling and scraping within his own wooden box—the man being so evil in life that his corporeal remains could find no peace in death. It must be said that spending six months in a tomb with only a handful of coffins to share your hideout would probably make anyone go mad, whether the deceased residents moved around or not.

Perhaps pheromones provide the most *rational* explanation and certainly hysteria whipped up by the theatrics of the tour guides cannot be discounted; fear is, afterall, said to be contagious and standing in the dead of night in an ancient graveyard would be enough to frighten most people even without dramatic tales of ghostly attacks from beyond the grave being whispered in your ear.

Maybe the truth is a combination of some—or even all—of the factors described above. Whatever the cause of the disturbances; ghosts, a poltergeist, elementals, the environment or even, as some visiting spiritualist mediums have claimed, the legacy of Satanist worship in the area, it is safe to say that the Black Mausoleum is a remarkable and intriguing addition to Edinburgh's already generous helping of ghoulish delights. As Jan-Andrew Henderson neatly put it:

> "Let me put it this way—if the Mackenzie Poltergeist isn't a genuine supernatural entity then I don't think there's any such thing. Not anywhere in the world."

3
The Sinister Secrets of Chambercombe Manor

Walled-up skeletons, ship-wreckers, pirates and a smorgasbord of ghostly goings-on.

Chambercombe Manor is a house of dark repute. Sections of this handsome building approach a thousand years old, reaching back to the Domesday Book and Norman rule. With a provenance of such age, there is a certain expectation that a house like this should have more than a few spooky tales to tell and in this the ghost hunter is not to be disappointed as the Manor is celebrated as being one of the most haunted properties in the British Isles, with a multitude of staff members and visitors having witnessed inexplicable and peculiar goings-on.

Located in the secluded Hele Valley in the seaside resort of Ilfracombe, North Devon, Chambercombe Manor belonged to the distinguished Champernon (or Champernowne) family from around 1160 until the mid-1300s when no male heir survived to inherit the estate. Ownership of it then passed through a variety of families; perhaps even that of Henry Grey, Duke of Suffolk (the father of the ill-fated Lady Jane Grey who was to reign as England's de facto monarch for nine days). Eventually, the house lost its connection to any noble estate and became a rather simpler farmhouse. Despite this separation, Chambercombe even now retains many reminders of its long history—some of which are, perhaps, of a non-corporeal nature.

The Manor's reputation as something of a hotspot for 'things that go bump in the night' has led to the property being visited on many occasions by paranormal research teams including Living TV's *Most Haunted* show. Indeed, Chambercombe plays host to regular ghost-themed events and there seems to be no end of strange phenomena to keep attendees both scared and intrigued. Of the many eye-witness reports, some stand out: a clock's pendulum has been observed to swing despite having no weights— and it has even toppled over during a tour; curtain poles have been seen to spin of their own accord, as has a 'meat jack' (or roasting spit) in the kitchen where the apparitions of a grey-clad lady, a "very unpleasant" man and a small boy are said to reside; visitors have reported being touched by an invisible entity that, it is also claimed, has pushed people out of chairs; and one man, Mr. Roger Watt, declared to have felt an invisible dog licking his leg in the Great Hall.

However, to use Chambercombe Manor expert Lesley Symons' words, this activity is merely "the tip of the iceberg", for the location seems to have an almost unending list of paranormal stirrings. Small objects move by themselves, doors become locked or slam shut seemingly without human interference, disembodied footsteps have been heard on many occasions, a multitude of 'cold spots' are often felt throughout the Manor's interior and the spirit of a man has been sensed near an old fireplace. As for visible apparitions, an old woman, dressed in black, sits ethereally on a downstairs windowsill while two young girls (one of whom is named 'Ellie') have been seen upstairs, either peering out from windows, sitting in the dressing room or lying on the Chippendale Room's bed. Additionally, a woman wearing a flowing white dress, and a horseman have both been sighted wandering in the grounds.

It's not just visible manifestations that the Manor is known for, for there are inexplicable smells that seem to permeate, from incense and floral aromas to rotting meat and even more stomach-churning scents.

Perhaps most chilling of all, though, is the apparition of a baby wrapped in swaddling clothes which has been seen lying in an old wooden cot. For extra spookiness, the cot sometimes rocks back-and-forth on its own. In this spot, there has also been seen a lady who seems to watch over the babe and an accompanying cold section of air that seems to defy explanation.

With such an abundance of phenomena, it's unsurprising that strange images are often captured on camera at Chambercombe. What's more, the Manor has attached to it one of the most interesting legends possessed by any of Britain's old houses—a legend that is linked to the notorious 'ship-wreckers' of Devon's past.

The earliest recording of this story seems to have appeared in the form of anonymous articles penned in 1865 and published in *The Leisure Hour*, a popular illustrated magazine that was printed in London and ran from 1852 until the end of the century. These articles were reprinted in the mid-1900s under the title *The Call of Chambercombe: A True Story of the North Devon Coast* with a preface written by the then owner of Chambercombe Manor, L.C.L. Pincombe. Pincombe wrote, "Like many other ancient buildings in this country, legends have become associated with the old Manor house which have been re-iterated for decades by folk of the neighbourhood and which, in more modern times, have found their way into print in a number of strange versions." Pincombe goes on to herald the following story as "a tribute to this author, whose name remains undiscovered despite many attempts to trace it".

The story begins with a traveller who, weary of the road and anxious to avoid nearby flooding, visited a pub called The Nag's Head. There, deep in conversation about local history with the landlord, he was shown two manuscripts which were supposedly discovered by the landlord's grandfather while he was working on a house close to Chambercombe Manor. The manuscripts told of a tale dating from 1663 about a young man named William Oatway. William's father, Alexander Oatway, owned Chambercombe Manor and was the leader of a group of notorious wreckers. Wreckers were opportunistic men who endeavoured to lure ships onto the dangerous rocks that make up parts of the Cornwall and Devon coasts, hoping that the vessels would founder and their passengers and cargos be washed up on shore where they could be robbed or stolen. They were dastardly men of larceny and, often, murder.

One night, young William rescued a girl who had been a passenger upon the wrecked ship *Granada*. Her name was Eleanor Gregory and, as Fate would have it, she and William would later marry. Before they could however, William was forced to flee his beloved Chambercombe, accused as an outlaw due to his father's association with the wreckers. He escaped to his late mother's family, eventually becoming a farmer, marrying Eleanor—who must have followed him at some point—and by all accounts doing quite well for himself.

With his criminal past long behind him, William went on to become something of a respected figure in his community and some years later he was asked to give up his farm and become the steward of Lundy Island which lies in the Bristol Channel, north of Devon. He accepted. The Island was sometimes subjected to the attentions of privateers and pirates due to the dangerous banks of shingle that forced commercial shipping into the safer waters around it, making it an excellent base from which to maraud the merchant ships and steal their valuable cargos.

One day, a French lieutenant called Reilland and his men tricked their way onto the Island by "bringing a coffin full of weapons ashore under the pretext that it contained the body of their dead captain". Despite killing most of the Island's inhabitants, Reilland and his pirates allowed William, Eleanor and their daughter Kate (a beautiful and spirited girl) to remain alive due to the intervention of one of their passengers, a Captain named Wallis. Wallis, (possibly possessing the forenames Duncan Tristian) an Irishman, fell in love with young Kate Oatway and they duly became man and wife, leaving Lundy to live in Wallis' native Dublin.

Many years later, William fulfilled his dream and he and Eleanor returned to Chambercombe as tenants, ever with the hope of once again owning the property outright. To that end, he planned to reopen the silver mine at Combe Martin which, though once productive, had since fallen into decline and eventually been abandoned entirely. Sadly though, William lacked the funds to spur his plan into action.

Then, in 1695, an opportunity to realise his dream presented itself. A powerful storm lashed the North Devon coast and William made his way down to the shore to see if any ships were in distress. Sure enough, past the wind-whipped spray and amid the churning waters, William could see a foundering ship. As he watched the ship break up, he noticed a bedraggled figure being washed onshore. It was a young woman and she was close to death, having been cruelly dashed upon the rocks. William carried her back to Chambercombe Manor where she soon died. As he searched her body for a clue to her identity, he found a money belt strapped around her waist: within, a great many gold coins. William, thinking that the gold could finance a reopening of the silver mine—or even buy the Manor outright—succumbed to temptation, stripped the dead woman of her accoutrements and kept her death a secret.

The next day, the ship's passenger list was found and taken to an Ilfracombe tavern where it was read out. There had been only a single woman registered onboard the ship: a Mrs. Katherine Wallis. William was drinking at the inn, no doubt quietly toasting his new-found fortune. He heard his daughter's name called out and, realising that he had robbed the corpse of his own darling child, became inconsolable with sorrow and remorse. He quickly returned home and laid Kate's body gently on a bed before sealing up the room. Eleanor passed away in the spring and, unable to go on living at Chambercombe, William leased out the estate to a tenant farmer and apparently spent the rest of his life "going about doing good".

It is a fascinating old legend, indeed, and the story doesn't stop there as many decades later (in 1865 or, possibly, 1738) the then occupant of Chambercombe, Jan Vye, made a discovery to make the heart race.

While undertaking repairs to the house, he noticed what appeared to be the faint outline of a bricked-up window and realised that inside the Manor there must exist a concealed chamber somewhere next to the Lady Jane Grey Room. Inside the house, Vye made an exploratory hole in the wall and with the aid of candlelight was confronted by a grisly sight. On a bedstead, in the middle of a small room, was a human skeleton.

The bones were identified as having belonged to a young woman, but beyond that no other details could be ascertained. Were these the last remains of William Oatway's beloved daughter? If so, why did he choose to abandon his daughter's body rather than seeing to it that she was buried in the proper fashion? What happened to the skeleton after it had been discovered? These questions—and more besides—remain.

Although many sources insist that Oatways once lived at the Manor, this author could find no official record to prove this.

In 1979 the Manor was donated to the Chambercombe Manor Trust and along with its extensive and delightful grounds it is now open to members of the public.

4

The Undead of the Underground

*What dark things have been unleashed beneath England's
venerable capital?*

The London Underground snakes its way through the
earth beneath one of the world's greatest capital cities. At
253 miles long and almost 150 years old, it is the second
longest and *the* oldest subterranean transport system in
existence. Some 270 stations punctuate its considerable
length and, in 2007 alone, a massive one billion passengers
were recorded to have used its services. But, the
Underground is more than just a bland transportation
network that ferries passengers to-and-fro via featureless
tunnels, for the vast complex through which the trains
speed has literally been carved through the macabre side of
Greater London's dark history, a fact that for some has left
an indelible and spectral stain upon the Tube.

And it isn't just the ancient dead that are associated
with the Underground, because within the labyrinthine
passageways that comprise it, thousands of unfortunate
souls have met a more recent end. Maintenance accidents,
murder, natural causes and even war have all cruelly
snatched life from some of those who work on or use the

network. Even the pitiless hand of terrorism has on occasion reached the snaking train tracks. Before the *'7th of July'* attacks, the Tube had been a popular target for the IRA and even the Suffragettes had a go back in 1913.

Of course, there are also the inevitable (and thankfully rare) accidents that pock-mark rail travel's safety records, but while fires, derailments and crashes have all caused regrettable deaths amongst commuters and workers alike, it is suicide that nestles forlornly atop the grim list. Indeed, many of the deeper stations have long depressions dug below the tracks to help stop people being run over if they fall off the platform (they were originally constructed as water drainage areas).

In spite of these pits—colloquially referred to as 'dead men's trenches'—suicide remains the highest cause of fatalities on the Tube, with as many as 150 attempts taking place over recent years: a third of which were 'successful'.

The Underground's morbid record stretches back much further than living memory. With a history spanning the best part of two thousand years, (reaching all the way back to 43 A.D. and the days of the Roman Empire,) London has been called home by countless numbers of people. As such, the earth below the modern-day city is made up of a multitude of layers that successive generations have laid down, and amongst the rubbish and rubble are hundreds of thousands—if not millions—of corpses.

The 1666 outbreak of the bubonic plague polished off some 100,000 unfortunate people: 20% of London's population at the time, and the large plague pits built to receive the victims' bodies have proved to be a major interference to subterranean constructions of all kinds.

Very few of these pits were accurately documented by contemporary records and many were sunk deeply into the earth to help combat the spread of infection. So, it was inevitable then, that any large-scale building works would lead to grisly discoveries and gruesome encounters—often without warning. *Unexplained Mysteries* columnist, Mike

Heffernan reveals more:

> "A huge tunnel-boring machine ploughed straight into a long-forgotten plague pit at Green Park, traumatising several brawny construction workers on-site."

Mike Heffernan's research goes on to describe how Liverpool Street station was constructed right on top of a plague pit, with a similar burial site existing behind a wall near the southern side of the Bakerloo Line's London road Depot. He also tells us how the Piccadilly Line between Knightsbridge and South Kensington is supposed to "curve around a pit so dense with human remains that it could not be tunnelled through."

So, plague pits, cemeteries and the dead resident therein have all been disturbed to make way for the meandering passageways of the Underground—it's no wonder that the network's tunnels and stations are said to be home to more than just staff and commuters.

Indeed, if all of the stories of phantoms are to be believed, the Underground is a veritable ghoul-filled warren...

Highgate High Level

Nestling between a pair of tunnels, Highgate High Level's empty platforms are situated directly above the Northern Line's modern Highgate station. Although long-closed to the public, local residents have reported the unmistakable clattering tumult of trains passing through the cutting. A claim made all the more intriguing by the fact that the overgrown station no longer has any tracks.

Becontree

Here doors rattle by themselves and several traumatised members of staff have told of being watched by a faceless woman with long blonde hair. She wears a white, ethereal dress and vanishes after only a few seconds but undoubtedly leaves a lasting impression.

Maida Vale

This Tube station was the first to be staffed by an entirely female workforce. Now though, it is notable for the disembodied hands that are supposed to make their presence known to commuters using the escalators that lead up to the street above.

British Museum

One of the Underground's oldest and most widely-known ghost stories is attached to the now defunct British Museum station. Formerly a bustling stop on the Central Line, this station's thirty-year lifespan came to an end in 1933 when nearby Holborn proved to be a better choice. Since then, a hush has settled upon its redundant platforms. That is, until nightfall when, emerging during the darkest hours, a long-deceased Egyptian princess is said to creep forth from a secret passageway that links the station with the world-renowned museum above it. Reports claim that wails and strange moans echo down the tunnels and sometimes even an intangible voice can be heard babbling in what might well be an ancient Egyptian tongue.

The pre-war British public became so fascinated by the rumour of an undead mummy roaming the tunnels that an unidentified newspaper offered a reward to anyone who would dare to spend a night in the darkened station. It seems that no brave soul volunteered to take up the challenge.

Aldwych

There are forty abandoned stations on the Underground network. While some have been left to decompose in darkness, others remain in surprisingly good condition and of those Aldwych is undoubtedly the most 'used' of London's disused tube stations.

Built upon the remains of the Royal Strand Theatre, the

station's working life came to an end in 1994 after 87 years servicing London's commuters. Now, its platforms and tunnels are something of a time capsule, used for private parties, music videos and even book launches. Films such as *28 Weeks Later*, *V for Vendetta* and *Patriot Games* have all made the most of Aldwych's classic London Underground backdrop, and fittingly, the phantom that is reputed to inhabit the station's dark recesses is said to be something of an actress herself.

Thought to have once trodden the boards of the Royal Strand Theatre, the female spectre has been spotted on the tracks by tunnel cleaners (named 'fluffers') and members of the public alike, but she managed to evade Living TV's *Most Haunted* crew, who spent twenty-four hours 'investigating' the station in 2002.

Bank

Another infamously spooky character, Sarah Whitehead, calls Bank home. The year 1812 saw the execution of her brother Philip. He had been accused by his employer, the Bank of England, of forgery and sentenced to be hanged in prison by an Old Bailey judge. The news of her brother's arrest, trial and execution was kept secret from Sarah and she only discovered the truth when she visited the Bank of England to enquire as to the whereabouts of Philip. It is said that the grim news only served to mentally unhinge her and she refused to accept that her brother was gone.

She took to wearing black attire from head to toe and would visit the Bank of England every day, searching for her sibling. She was soon given the nickname the 'Bank Nun'.

Eventually, the governors became fed up with her eccentricities and decided to offer her a sum of money if she agreed to never return, which she acceded to. In death, however, she apparently does to return, replete in black clothes and sometimes surprising late night travellers by approaching them and asking if they have seen her brother.

Sarah's coal-black apparition has also been seen on more than one occasion in the Bank garden (she was buried there when the garden used to be a churchyard), while on Bank's platforms and in its corridors, commuters and workers have often reported mysterious and foul smells, overwhelming feelings of sadness and anxiety, and even a bizarre sense of hopelessness (although it must be said that these are emotions that some commuters also feel on the Tube, without paranormal assistance). Some people look to Sarah's story as the origin of the Bank of England's nick-name 'the Old Lady of Threadneedle Street'.

Adding to Bank's macabre ambience is the fact that the current ticket hall is situated where a crypt used to be...

Farringdon

Poor Annie Naylor, an apprentice milliner and barely thirteen years old when she was cruelly beaten, starved and eventually murdered by her hat-making employer Sarah Metyard and her daughter Sarah Morgan Metyard in 1758. Four years later, and the murderous Metyards were apprehended and sentenced to hang at Tyburn before being publicly dissected. The building in which the infanticide happened was one of those demolished to make way for Farringdon Station which opened in 1863. Annie's blood-curdling screams are occasionally heard resonating through the tunnels by open-mouthed passengers. So loud are they that staff have named her 'the Screaming Spectre'.

Hyde Park Corner

Lying on the Piccadilly Line, sandwiched between Green Park and Knightsbridge, Hyde Park Corner Station is notable for being one of the rare stops on the network to have no corresponding buildings above ground. It is also distinguished for the terrifying experience that two of its workers endured during one November night-shift in 1978.

Station supervisor Barry Oakley and an anonymous colleague had closed the station down for the night and shut off the escalators before returning to Oakley's office. In the early hours of the morning, the two men were alarmed by the sound of some kind of commotion emanating from the booking hall. Their hasty investigation revealed that the noise had come from the escalators coming back on—a fact most peculiar considering that they had been disconnected from the electrical supply and needed a specific key to be reactivated. A "thorough but fruitless" search revealed nothing out of the ordinary and the two men walked back to Oakley's office just after 3 o'clock in the morning. Soon after returning, the room became inexplicably cold, so cold in fact that Mr. Oakley could see his breath when making tea for them both. When he turned around to face his unusually quiet colleague, Oakley saw immediately that the colour had completely drained from his friend's face and he was looking utterly terrified. When prompted for an explanation, the colleague simply asked whether the station supervisor had seen "the face". According to the man, a ghostly face and head had come through one of the walls and "spent some time staring at the pair of them". The colleague was visibly shaken and went home early, never to return to work on the Tube again.

Covent Garden

Reports of ghostly activity here stretch back to the 1950s. Strange noises and phantom footsteps are said to echo along the platforms, but it is the ghost of swash-buckling and Shakespearean actor William Terriss (born William Charles James Lewin) that has caused the most commotion over the years. Appearing mostly in November and December, Terriss' apparition materialises in an old-fashioned grey frock coat and gloves and peers about before vanishing. Perhaps something about the station is linked to his murder by Richard Archer Prince, an impoverished actor who stabbed the well-liked Terriss in a jealous rage in 1897.

Kennington Loop

The Loop is a long, horseshoe-shaped section of track underneath south London that was put in place to make it possible for trains to turn around and head back north. No passengers are allowed here and people are unable to get onto the trains or off them. Which makes it all the more interesting that the Loop is said to have such a great deal of incidents of a supernatural nature.

After the carriages are checked for passengers the trains make their way into the Loop, sometimes waiting in the darkness for twenty minutes or more (in complete silence) while the platform ahead is cleared. It is then that the strange things are said to take place. Weird emotions, the sounds of disembodied conversations taking place and— perhaps most frighteningly—doors repeatedly slamming, are all reported to have happened here on more than one occasion. The doors that slam are those that lie between the carriages and some drivers have reported hearing them opening and closing along the train's length, getting closer and closer to the driver as though someone were walking hastily through the carriages towards them. It's no wonder that staff are said to heartily dislike the Kennington Loop.

Elephant & Castle

Tapping noises, a runner's echoing footsteps and doors opening of their own accord make the Elephant & Castle's platforms eerie places to wander through at night. These footsteps are thought to belong to the spectral girl that sometimes enters the trains and likes to walk through the carriages before disappearing.

But not all of the strange phenomena associated with the Underground are tethered to the Tube's scores of stations. For instance, quite a number of (mainly) northbound passengers on the Bakerloo Line have reported glimpsing the ghostly reflection in the carriage window of someone reclining in the seat next to them even though it is very much vacant. Others have reported a spectral face staring at them after speeding away from Elephant & Castle. Diggers during the 1960s working near Vauxhall's station on the Victoria Line told of sightings of a strange figure, possibly a ghostly workman of seven-feet-tall, clad in brown overalls and a flat cap.

Reports of spectral monks walking along the tracks of the Jubilee Line have been related since the line's opening in 1979; perhaps they are connected to the large number of graves that were disturbed during construction.

Still on the Jubilee Line, an experienced patrolman was walking the track between Baker Street station and St. John's Wood station when he heard the rhythmic crunch of footsteps approaching him from the darkness ahead. He scanned the tunnel with his torch, but could see nothing that might explain the sound until, to his horror, he saw "heavy footsteps crunching down on the ballast between the railway sleepers"—as if made by an invisible man. Rigid with fear, the patrolman watched open-mouthed as the steps continued past him and on up the tunnel the way he had come. Upon relating his frightening tale, he discovered that he was not alone in witnessing the phenomenon: many colleagues of his had quietly endured the same experience. Records indicate that five members of various maintenance crews have been killed at that section of the line over the years.

A manager-in-training was walking the Northern Line near Stockwell Station when he encountered an old man he did not recognise working at South Island Place which is a 'step-plate junction'. The stranger was carrying an out-moded Tilly lamp for illumination. The manager asked the man the name of the place and why he was using the old lamp. The old man replied, giving the name as South Island Place, and said that he preferred his oil-burning lamp to those "new-fangled electric torches".

Leaving the man to his work, and continuing on his

way, the manager reached Stockwell and related his curious encounter to staff there. No maintenance work was scheduled to be carried out at that section so a search party was assembled and set off to look for the man carrying the lamp. Despite scouring the area twice and delaying the start of service, no old man could be found in the tunnels. Many more workers have spotted the old man with the Tilly lamp over the years. A track worker was killed near South Island Place in the 1950s when the "compressor he was working on drowned out the sound of an approaching train" and he was run over. Perhaps this is the lingering spirit with the Tilly lamp.

And of course, there is the magnificent legend—of dubious and mysterious origin, it must be said—that describes a group of humans who began to live in the warren of tunnels that make up the Underground sometime in the late 19th century. Now mutated or devolved, these subterranean beings, or 'Morlocks', survive by scavenging for food that has been discarded by careless commuters.

Some even say that the odd late-night traveller occasionally augments their diet...

5
The Ghoul of Hampton Court Palace

The camera never lies: was a bona fide phantom caught on film at this royal residence?

Eager sightseers are not the only visitors to this historic and beautiful palace. Like many old buildings scattered around the British Isles, Hampton Court Palace harbours multitudinous tales of otherworldly inhabitants—dark entities that creep along its passageways; spiritual relics of a bygone age that supposedly linger on after death and occasionally surprise the unsuspecting visitor.

Jane Seymour is said to wander the Clock Court, ethereal in a floating white gown and carrying a flickering candle. Catherine Howard has been seen on numerous occasions in the appropriately named Haunted Gallery. Long-dead Cavaliers have been perceived wandering the Palace's grounds and, of course, Cardinal Wolsey's spectre is said to still walk through the edifice's aged but splendid corridors.

The first buildings at the Hampton Court Palace site were constructed in the 12th century by the Knights Hospitallers of St John of Jerusalem. Over the following centuries the location grew to become an important, lavish and royal centre within whose walls walked such illustrious characters from Britain's history as Henry VIII, Elizabeth I, James I and Charles I. The buildings; opulent and sumptuous, were strictly off-limits to the British public until 1838 when, in the first year of her reign, the young Queen Victoria, ordered that Hampton Court Palace be thrown open to all her subjects without restriction. Since then, thousands of visitors have flocked to the Palace and it has become one of Britain's most popular tourist attractions.

Recently however, the Palace played host to an event that brought with it a new claim to fame.

Three times over consecutive days in October of 2003, members of the Palace's security staff were called to attend to one particular fire door near the Introductory Exhibition. On the first day, members of staff were alerted when alarms began ringing—an indication that a secured door had been opened without authorisation. Staff members visited the fire door in question and, finding it to be open, made sure it was re-closed securely. There was no other suspicious activity to report and nothing else seemed to be out of place. A review of the footage from a closed-circuit television camera (well-positioned opposite and above the doorway) showed the doors opening "with great force", but no human presence or natural occurrence to explain why. This took place around 1pm.

The next day hosted similar events, but this time there was a shock in store for staff members. Once again, alarm bells signalled the impromptu opening of the fire door. Another trip out to the doors in question revealed that this time they were closed. The CCTV was viewed for a second time. As before, it had captured the flinging open of the double doors, but this time something extra was caught on camera: a curious figure could be seen stepping forward into the vacant door frame, grasping the door handles and sharply pulling them closed. The figure, though grainy, could clearly be seen dressed in a long, furred-trimmed coat with flowing cuffs and a high collar (or perhaps ruff): unusual apparel indeed.

The next day's activity compounded the mystery. The same doors flew open once again at the same time as they had done before. As with the first two incidents, no reason for the doorway's abrupt opening could be found and nothing unusual had been spotted by anybody nearby, nor did the odd figure reappear on the CCTV footage.

A security guard at the Palace is quoted by the UK Press Association as saying:

> "I was shocked when the CCTV footage showed an eerie figure in period dress in the doorway. It was incredibly spooky because the face just didn't look human. My first reaction was that someone was having a laugh, so I asked my colleagues to take a look. We spoke to our costumed guides but they don't own a costume like that worn by the figure. It is actually quite unnerving!"

It is claimed that some Australian tourists came forward to say that they too had seen a ghost near the exhibition area near the time in question. Similarly, an entry in the Palace's visitor comments book stated that a sightseer thought she had seen some kind of apparition in the same location.

Hampton Court Palace has often used costumed guides to augment their tours, and this would seem to offer an obvious and earthly explanation for the apparition, but the possibility that these theatrical figures could have been mistaken for a phantom has been eliminated as the guides do not enter the part of the building in question. Indeed, as the quote above maintains, they do not even possess costumes such as that worn by the figure in the CCTV footage.

Some sceptics have asked if the ghost of a person who lived hundreds of years ago could possibly know how to operate a modern fire door, and even opined that the figure looks too real—too solid—to be an apparition. The website Paranormal-Investigation.com reviewed the footage and concluded:

> "When enhanced and stabilized, the video looks far less like a ghost and more like an attendant of some kind who is wearing period costume. The press and media took the most ghost-like image of the low resolution sequence and circulated the low resolution and shaky images from video without any processing to balance contrast and used this to claim it was a ghost, but when you look at the sequence once enhanced and stabilized it looks less convincing.
>
> "Would a 17th century spirit know how to operate a fire exit door? I'm sure most modern people have difficulty closing them but the 'ghost' seemed quite able to get it to work, closing one side then the other. The motion of the legs, arms and hands appear totally solid and are consistent with that of known human articulation."

Of course, it is important to analyse footage like this, but in this case it is a little too harsh. When the vast majority of 'ghost photographs' are dismissed as indistinguishable and indefinite, it is refreshing to have a more substantial-looking recording to view, at the very least. Furthermore, who is to say how solid a ghost should look, or whether a representative of the spirit-world would indeed be able to interact fluently with modern objects or not?

A scarcity of information has been released officially by Hampton Court Palace (beyond the main, regurgitated facts that every website reproduces about the incident).

Interestingly, it took months for the staff to release the CCTV tape to the public after the strange image was captured mainly because the now infamous fire door had a history of being opened without authorisation, thus causing alarms to go off.

Internal memos had been circulated amongst the staff to stop what was believed to be a troublemaker from tampering with the door, however, no wrongdoer was found until the video appeared to show that the robed figure had been responsible for setting off the alarms on at least one occasion. Even then, an earthly perpetrator was still suspected and an investigation initiated, but when the inquiry failed to bear fruit the footage was released to a wider audience.

"We're baffled too; it's not a joke, we haven't manufactured it," said Hampton Court spokeswoman Vikki Wood when asked whether the CCTV footage was a hoax or not, "we genuinely don't know who it is or what it is."

Psychologist Dr. Richard Wiseman stated that the spectre, which has now been given the moniker 'Skeletor', might prove to be a significant breakthrough: "It could be the best ghost sighting ever," he said, adding, "I haven't seen anything that would match that at all". This is, of course, if the figure really is a bona fide apparition. Dr. Wiseman also gave his opinion on what the figure is most likely to be, remarking that "It is either a publicity stunt by the Palace, which I doubt, or it is a member of the public thinking they were being helpful by shutting the doors."

Security staff members at the Palace remain adamant that it is not a deception and while providing a new point of interest, it would hardly have increased the Palace's profits by much, especially considering its long list of pre-existing hauntings and that no new ghostly merchandise or publications have been issued to profit from the CCTV footage.

And so it is doubtful whether the figure will ever be proved as a genuine ghost or not, but certainly the footage makes for transfixing viewing and, to this day, there are some employees who are reluctant to spend time in the exhibition area after dark.

6
The Horror of the Hairy Hands

On a lonely road across Dartmoor, a violent spectre sends travellers veering off the road and, sometimes, to their graves...

Dartmoor: almost a thousand square kilometres of bleak, elemental land. Here, amid the regal menhirs, rocky tors and dangerous bogs, fairytales and legends flourish and have done so for many hundreds of years, with spectral hounds, pixies and even a decapitated horseman all thought by some to roam this vast, desolate moorland.

It is to a quite precise point in Dartmoor that we turn our attention; a stretch of road where a truly horrifying apparition has reportedly been the reason behind a multitude of accidents—some of them sadly fatal.

The road that links the small villages of Postbridge and Two Bridges is an old one. Now assigned the name B3212, it was once a turnpike (toll road) named Carter's Road and was built in the late 18th century. For a long time it was the only 'proper' route to cross the moor's earthy expanse. In more recent times, a short section of this thoroughfare has become known as a particularly spooky 'accident black spot', the cause of which has a most unusual and unique attribution.

Since the early years of the 1900s, motorists and cyclists using this road near Postbridge have sometimes reported a sudden loss of control of their vehicle. The cause? Their steering wheels or handlebars being wrenched from their grasp by a pair of hirsute disembodied hands! No matter how hard they struggled against the bizarre 'Hairy Hands', their vehicles usually ended up driven off the road. Even horses and carts suffered a similar fate.

In June of 1921, Dr. E.H. Helby, who worked as a medical officer at HM Prison Dartmoor, was killed after his motorcycle uncontrollably veered off the road and crashed. On the approach to the small bridge there, he had shouted to the two children who were riding in the motorcycle's sidecar (the daughters of Dartmoor Prison's governor) to jump clear. Thankfully, the young girls managed to do just that, but the doctor was less fortunate and the ensuing crash brought about his premature death.

In fact, 1921 was to prove a busy year for the Hairy Hands as just a few weeks after Dr. Helby's demise a coach driver experienced a similar loss of control when his vehicle skidded off the road, injuring some of the passengers in the process. Then, on the 26th of August, a captain of the British Army crashed his motorcycle at the exact same spot. Despite most sources maintaining that the unnamed captain died, the following quote from said captain seems to suggest otherwise:

> "It was not my fault. Believe it or not, something drove me off the road. A pair of hairy hands closed over [my own]. I felt them as plainly as ever I felt anything in my life— large, muscular, hairy hands. I fought them for all I was worth, but they were too strong for me. They forced the machine into the turf at the edge of the road, and I knew no more till I came-to myself, lying a few feet away on my face, on the turf."

Naturally, the area quickly became notorious and stories of the Hairy Hands even made it into the national newspapers.

Ghost Club investigator Michael Williams' book, *Supernatural Dartmoor*, hosts an anecdote recounted by the writer Ronald 'Rufus' Endle, who died in 1986. In it, Endle tells how he was driving his car near Postbridge when "A pair of hands gripped the driving wheel and I had to fight for control." Endle was lucky (or strong enough) and was able to maintain control of his car before the hands disappeared "as inexplicably as they had come". Interestingly, Endle supposedly asked Michael Williams to hold the story back from publication at least until after his death, presumably out of fear of ridicule.

Another instance involved a lady by the name of Florence Warwick who was on holiday in south Devon. While travelling along the B3212 to her accommodation in Torbay after a sightseeing trip, the 28-year-old woman's car unexpectedly shuddered to a halt near Postbridge and refused to restart. Warwick leaned over and delved into the glove-box to retrieve the car's manual. She said:

> "As I was reading in the failing light, a cold feeling suddenly came over me. I felt as if I was being watched. I looked up and saw a pair of huge, hairy hands pressed against the windscreen. I tried to scream, but couldn't. I was frozen with fear."

Terrifyingly, the hands proceeded to crawl across the screen by themselves:

> "It was horrible—they were just inches away. After what seemed a lifetime, I heard myself cry out and the hands seemed to vanish."

Luckily, a frantic attempt to start the car's engine was

successful and she sped off to safety. Supposedly, Florence Warwick had not known about the tales of the Hairy Hands before her encounter with them and it was only after she related her terrifying experience to friends that she was told about the old legend.

Another fatal crash happened in 1960 when a car left the road and overturned. The driver had been making his way from Plymouth to Chagford when he mysteriously lost control of the car. No evidence of the involvement of another vehicle was found and the police investigation found no mechanical problems with the car itself.

Motorists are not the only ones to have suffered unwanted attention from this most unusual manifestation. Hikers walking close to this notorious section of road have claimed "strange experiences and sensations".

In the rather wet summer of 1924, Theo Brown, the popular folklorist, was sleeping in her caravan (possibly the famous 'Loiterer'), not far from the B3212 when she sensed that something was afoot:

> "As I looked up to the little window at the end of the caravan, I saw something moving, and as I stared, I saw it was the fingers and palm of a very large hand with many hairs on the joints and back of it, clawing up and up to the top of the window, which was a little open. I knew it wished to do harm to my husband sleeping below. I knew that the owner of the hand hated us and wished harm, and I knew it was no ordinary hand, and that no blow or shot would have any power over it.
>
> "Almost unconsciously I made the Sign of the Cross and I prayed very much that we might be kept safe. At once the hand slowly sank down out of sight and I knew the danger was gone. I did say a thankful prayer and fell at once into a peaceful sleep.

"We stayed in that spot for several weeks but I never felt the evil influence again near the caravan. But, I did not feel happy in some places not far off and would not for anything have walked alone on the moor at night or on the Tor above our caravan."

If, as some sources suggest, Theo Brown's caravan had been parked amongst the scattered remnants of Powder Mills (once a thriving industrial site, but now a series of ruined buildings slowly being reclaimed by the moor), the tor mentioned above must be Higher White Tor. Powder Mills itself is an interesting location for one of the few stories that claims to shed light upon the Hairy Hands' origin is set there.

During the second half of the 1800s, the Plymouth and Dartmoor Gunpowder Company's Powder Mills was a busy complex that attempted to satisfy the area's great demand for gunpowder. This explosive was needed not just for blasting rock at the local quarries, but also by farms with rocky enclosures that required clearing. Naturally, the risk of explosion at the mill was ever-present and all measures to avoid naked flames and accidental sparks were undertaken by the workers. This even included the removal of metal studs from the soles of their boots lest they strike against rough ground and create sparks.

The local blacksmith who—conveniently enough—is said to have possessed "big strong, hairy arms and hands", was contracted to repair the Mill's faulty machinery. The story goes that one evening, after more than a few drinks, the burly smith wandered up to the Mill having forgotten to take off his hob-nailed boots. As his soles struck the granite floor, the ensuing sparks ignited some nearby gunpowder and exploded, vapourising most of the hapless man. The story closes by saying that only his hands were found intact...

Other explanations discount the blacksmith's legend and say that the mutilated hands belong to an unnamed man who expired in an accident on the road, although further details are elusive. Still others point to an ancient Bronze Age settlement that once existed in that area of Dartmoor and a legend that now seems to be lost.

Whatever the origin, the police have never seemed to take the supernatural aspects of the reports seriously and even local residents mainly blamed drunkenness or unfamiliarity with the slim Dartmoor roads for the accidents, especially when the 'victim' turned out to be a 'grockle' (Devon slang for 'tourist').

Investigations undertaken by the local council in recent years revealed that the road had a slightly unusual camber, which was subsequently rectified. Furthermore, harsher speed limits were introduced in an attempt to protect drivers and the free-roaming livestock from life-threatening collisions.

For now, the hideous Hairy Hands seem to have disappeared. Or perhaps they are still out there somewhere on the desolate moor, lying in wait..

7

The Monster of Glamis Castle

What dreadful secret haunts the Earls of Strathmore?

The imposing, baronial figure of Glamis Castle is a striking vision to behold. With its long, arrow-straight driveway, plentiful turrets, crenellated battlements and shining, latticed windows it has everything you could wish for from a Scottish castle. But the beautifully-restored architecture isn't the only notable feature of Glamis, for, like every good castle, it has a long history punctuated with darkness.

It was perhaps fitting then, that the celebrated playwright William Shakespeare used Glamis as a backdrop for Macbeth, one of his most sinister plays. And what an apt setting it makes, for the Castle is reputed to be the most haunted in the whole of Scotland.

Old legends and stories surround Glamis and tell of eldritch things such as the dark apparitions that are supposed to stalk the edifice's many passageways and extensive grounds. Among them: a grey lady, said to be the ghost of Lady Janet Douglas who was accused of sorcery and burned at the stake as a witch; an unidentified serving woman with no tongue who wanders the Castle's grounds plucking at her disfigured mouth in distress—occasionally she is also seen peering out from a barred window and gazing forlornly at onlookers below; and of course, the cruel and notorious gambler Earl Beardie (more on him later).

But amongst this assortment of spectres there is one that haunts this, the family home of the Earls of Strathmore & Kinghorne and the childhood residence of the late Queen Mother, more than any other...the Monster of Glamis.

As with so many similar stories, the Monster is really a man. The tale goes that a hideously deformed boy was born at Glamis to a member of the Bowes-Lyon family. So unsightly was the boy that he was not expected to live, but he surprised the family, not only by surviving infancy, but by growing into maturity and even coming to possess considerable size and strength. It was quickly decided that his existence should become a closely-guarded secret and that only the Earl, his heir (upon reaching his twenty-first birthday), and Glamis' factor (the person charged with managing the estate) were to know of the infant's being. He was nursed through childhood and adolescence in strict concealment and kept locked away in a hidden room somewhere in Glamis.

Removed from the world's gaze, he was fed via a metal grille and let out only rarely for exercise—and even then only when darkness had fallen and the moon was hidden behind thick clouds. The Queen Mother's biographer, James Wentworth Day, gives us this description of him: "His chest an enormous barrel, hairy as a doormat, his head ran straight into his shoulders and his arms and legs were toy-like." While that expert on all things paranormal, Peter Underwood, portrayed him as looking like, "an enormous flabby egg".

In spite of attempts to keep knowledge of the Monster's presence limited to but a handful of people, local rumours of the deformed baby's survival sprang forth. These could have originated with the midwife who had overseen delivery of the baby boy because, she alleged that though deformed, he was in 'rude health' when she had last seen him, and she had been surprised to hear his death announced soon after. Also, some sources believe that, oddly, no gravestone was erected for the baby. Old wives' tales endure to this day about how this 'creature' would be occasionally glimpsed wandering in the woods and by the waterways, always walking with great clumsiness and never without a chaperone. There was even talk of local prostitutes being handsomely paid to visit the Monster, although this is rather unbelievable if the family wanted the secret to remain as such.

Thanks to years of research, there is a fairly strong candidate for the identity of Glamis' frightful enigma: the first-born son of Thomas Lyon-Bowes, Lord Glamis. Thomas, who was the eldest son of the 11th Earl of Strathmore and Kinghorne, married Miss Charlotte Grimstead on the 21st of December, 1820. Charlotte quickly became pregnant and they had their first child—a son named after its father, on the 18th of October, 1821. Alas, the baby died the same day (a fact backed up by Sir Robert Douglas's *Peerage of Scotland*, *Cracroft's Peerage* and George Edward Cokayne's *The Complete Peerage*). Next year the couple had a second son, and chose to use the father's forename once again, this time calling the baby Thomas George.

So, while there is no evidence from the peerages that the short-lived first son was disabled or deformed, they do at least offer up the most likely identity for the Monster— if, of course, the legend is to be believed.

Thomas George inherited the title and estates upon his grandfather's death in 1846. A keen cricketer, he married a woman called Charlotte Maria Barrington but, for some reason, Thomas and his wife never had children themselves. Perhaps knowledge and fear of more 'monstrous' offspring stopped him from attempting issue. Thomas George died childless in September of 1865, and his younger brother Claude succeeded him to become the 13th Earl of Strathmore. Claude was, by all accounts, a kind and conscientious family man. From the day of his succession, though, a startling change befell the new Earl. He became suddenly serious and withdrawn, even mentioning to his wife on one occasion that although they had often joked about Glamis' 'monstrous' secret, his views upon it had changed dramatically since assuming his family's burdens: "I have been into the room, I have heard the secret, and if you wish to please me you will never mention the subject again."

A similar quote to the one above is given by James Wentworth Day, but this time the words are attributed to Andrew Ralston, the estate's factor in the latter half of the 1800s until his death in 1914. Cecilia Bowes-Lyon (the Countess of Strathmore and Queen Elizabeth II's maternal grandmother) had heard the rumours of the Monster's existence and attempted to extract the details from Andrew Ralston. He told her in no uncertain terms that, "It is fortunate you do not know the truth, for, if you did, you would never spend another night beneath this roof."

Another factor (or perhaps the same one) was invited by his Earl to sleep in the castle overnight as a winter snowstorm had begun to swirl violently outside. Despite being described as a stout fellow, the factor declined the offer and decided that braving the storm was a preferable course of action to staying overnight at Glamis. When the Earl's wife questioned him as to why he wouldn't sleep in the castle he replied, "Madame, I cannot tell, else you wouldn't sleep anymore."

Furthermore, James Wentworth Day goes on to give an account of the discovery by a workman of a secret passage within the castle, supposedly near to the chapel. Bravely (or foolishly), the workman explored it and stumbled upon something that frightened him greatly. The Earl, who was away at the time, was immediately informed of the workman's discovery via telegram. He returned to Glamis from London (or perhaps Edinburgh, as some writers say) with his lawyer in tow, halted the renovations there and then, and questioned the workman in private. The result of this was that the man seems to have been bribed into silence and paid to emigrate halfway across the planet to Australia—with the vast sum of several hundred thousand pounds in his bank account. Incidentally, Lord Halifax (Charles Wood, 2nd Viscount Halifax) suggests that the 'workman' incident happened in 1875.

Another 'close shave' came when a group of guests attempted to find the secret room by bribing the staff to turn a blind eye while they hung towels and sheets out of every window they could find. From the castle grounds they found that a number of windows were without material (some say four rooms in total). Again, the Earl at the time was away on business but returned early enough to angrily put a stop to the search and throw them all out before the hidden rooms could be traced.

But, what if the Monster isn't a man at all? Over the years, there have been many suggestions as to what was inside that hidden room.

One of the most fantastical versions of the legend maintains that women of the Bowes-Lyon family occasionally give birth to vampires and that the secret room is where these blood-sucking offspring are kept alive in isolation.

Another account has it that the room in question plays host to the damned spirit of Earl Beardie. Beardie, who is either Alexander Lyon, 2nd Lord Glamis or Alexander Lindsay, 4th Earl of Crawford, was a man of rambunctious character. Late one Saturday night, when the Sabbath neared, he became angry that he could find nobody with whom to play cards. Gambling on a Sunday was much frowned upon and no man was prepared to join the irate Earl in his drunken games. Beardie swore that if nobody had the courage to take him on he would gladly play with the Devil himself. At that instant a mysterious, dark stranger appeared at the castle door and, having heard Beardie's words, offered to join him for a game or two. The Earl readily agreed and so the two men played. As the game progressed, the stakes grew higher and higher and

Beardie lost more and more, until finally he was playing for his very soul. Beardie lost, the stranger vanished and the drunken Earl was doomed to play out his sacrilegious gambling for eternity in Glamis' hidden room.

Of course, alongside the myths and legends, lie more scientifically sound explanations for the Monster. It is quite possible that a child was born with physical deformities that were not understood or sympathised with at the time. The baby could have suffered from any of a large array of rare disorders, among them: quadramembral limb deficiency, which results in shortened arms and legs and would go some way to explaining Peter Underwood's 'oviform' description of the Monster above. The child could even have inherited a variety of genetic disorders such as Neurofibromatosis Type I and Proteus Syndrome as Joseph Merrick was now thought by some to have suffered from. Superstition, pride, religious beliefs or a combination of all three could have caused the family to think their infant son was ill-fitting to be part of such a noble family and, when he survived childbirth unexpectedly, they could only think to lock him away.

Anthony D. Hippisley-Coxe suggests an historical reason for the secret in his book *Haunted Britain*. He writes that the hidden room might contain: "incriminating evidence against Mary, Queen of Scots", whatever that may be.

Another theory with historical roots suggests that Glamis' hidden room contained neither a monster nor a man, but instead evidence of an ancient mass murder. The story goes that a party of Ogilvies, fleeing their enemies, came to Glamis seeking sanctuary. But alas, the Ogilvies found no asylum at the Castle, for they were herded into a secret room, the door locked and barricaded behind them, and then left there to starve to death. Their skeletons might even remain in the room to this day.

What's perhaps more puzzling than the nature of the legend itself is that if the Earls of Strathmore took such pains to ensure the truth remained covert, why then do we know so much about the legend now? Well, unexpectedly, much of the information seems to have come straight from members of the Bowes-Lyon family themselves. James Wentworth Day's biography of the Queen Mother included a "revealing account" of the monster legend and provided much of the information that is currently in the public domain. He also mentioned that his informant was "a member of the Queen Mother's family". Tantalising speculation about whether that source was actually the Queen Mother herself was common at the time.

But, perhaps the Monster has always simply been an exercise in 'smoke and mirrors'—a way to hide a guilt darker than any legend. After all, the story of a monster contained with a hidden chamber is not restricted to Glamis: the ruined Castle of Vayne, which lies a little to the north of Glamis, is said to stand upon a dungeon filled with ancient treasures and guarded by an "uncouth monster in the shape of a horned ox"; while even further north is Fyvie Castle, where a secret room in the south west corner of the tower remains closed because "disaster befalls any who enter". Perchance, the legend is one in which an existing story has been embellished and transformed over the centuries for entertainment, mischief or simply hearsay.

Glamis itself claims no official knowledge of the legend at all and, although it is proud of the myriad ghosts that are said to walk its corridors and gardens, this lack of acknowledgement of the Monster is a mystery in itself considering that the story of the Monster of Glamis Castle is a frequent addition to the numerous of books and web sites that are interested in such things.

Perhaps though, it is fitting if the final words on Glamis Castle are given to David Lindsay, the cultured Earl of Crawford. After a visit to the castle, he noted in his diary: "As to the alleged secret, I soon fathomed the mystery. There is a secret: the secret is that there is no secret."

8

The Mysterious Mongoose of Cashen's Gap

*A talking mongoose that seemed to possess astonishing powers
became an international sensation, but what was there any
truth behind this bizarre creature?*

The weird and wonderful story of the Isle of Man's
baffling 'mongoose' began in the latter half of 1931. Up a
steep incline on an exposed hillside two miles from the
small village of Dalby stood a farmhouse named Cashen's
Gap (or *Doarlish Cashen* in the Manx Gaelic language). It
was an austere-looking abode, set upon a bleak
prominence where neither electricity nor the telephone
reached. Ahead stretched the Irish Sea, and Ireland's misty
shore was just visible from the farmhouse on clear days.
The famous psychic researcher Harry Price, who would
later visit Cashen's Gap, described it as "one of the
loneliest farmsteads in Britain, seeming to lie upon the
roof of the world, and in midwinter, shrinks within itself,
shivering under the continual lash of wind and rain."

The farm was home to a man named James Irving, his
wife Margaret and one of their daughters, Voirrey (a Manx
version of the name Mary, and pronounced to rhyme with
'sorry',) who was twelve or thirteen at the time. In the

September of 1931, the family began to hear strange noises inside the house: "barking, growling, spitting and persistent blowing like a weasel". The sounds seemed to come from the spaces behind the wooden matchboard panels that were fixed to the interior walls to help insulate the house against the island's harsh weather.

The noises persisted. Eventually, James decided to set traps in an attempt to catch the animal, even resorting to laying down poison, but no creature could be caught, alive or dead. Initially, the Irvings assumed a rodent or a similar small animal had somehow found a way to enter the slim spaces behind the panels, but soon, whatever it was began to make some shockingly unrodent-like sounds.

It started by copying the animal noises that it heard, repeating growls, barks and tweets with an astonishingly accurate talent for mimicry. Soon, James found that "he had only to *name* an animal and [the creature] would promptly respond with the appropriate imitation". Even more amazingly, it wasn't long until the thing began to make baby-like noises, as though it was experimenting with human language. It was. Its progress was rapid. By November it was quite accomplished at speaking English and could talk in a high, screechy sort of voice, conversing readily with the Irving family and even singing nursery rhymes. Much of what it said would be preserved in contemporary accounts, letters and interviews.

It said that its name was 'Gef' (pronounced with a soft 'G'), even spelling it out for the Irvings. Naturally, the family was flabbergasted. In a letter, James wrote of his feelings about Gef: "Whatever Gef is, animal only, or spirit in this form, there has never, I am sure, been anything like it on this earth before."

In time, Gef showed himself to the family, but only ever wholly to Voirrey; James and Margaret could barely seem to catch fleeting glimpses of him. According to the young girl, whatever kind of animal the creature was, he was about the size of a rat with fur of a yellow colour and a large bushy tail.

Gef described himself variously as "an extra, extra clever mongoose", an "earthbound spirit," and "a ghost in the form of a weasel". He claimed to possess great powers and said that even though he wasn't an evil entity, he could be malevolent if he so desired. He told James Irving that "you don't know what damage or harm I could do if I were roused. I could kill you all—but I won't." In fact, Gef was said to remain mostly amicable towards the family and assured them that if they were kind to him he would bring them 'good luck'.

He made his home in a small section of Voirrey's modest bedroom, naming it his 'sanctum' and, despite allegedly saying "I have been to nicer homes than this. Carpets, piano, satin covers on polished tables," he seemed content to be in Cashen's Gap. "This is my home, it suits me." he said on one occasion. When asked to list the reasons for his contentedness, he said "I have three attractions. I follow Voirrey, Mam gives me food, and Jim answers my questions."

Gef would often bring rabbits home for Margaret to cook and was sometimes rewarded with bananas, biscuits, sweets and chocolate. He was also fond of bacon and sausages. The food would be placed upon the wooden beams underneath the ceiling and the mongoose would creep out to snatch it away when nobody was looking. Gef enjoyed singing as much as talking. One of his favourite tunes was a popular 1928 Gene Austin song called *Carolina Moon* which he would sometimes bounce a rubber ball along to. He also sang the Manx national anthem, several hymns and "some fragments of a Spanish folksong".

But Gef was also ill-tempered and mischievous and from time-to-time he would torment his human house-mates, throwing stones at Margaret as she walked home across the fields and rough tracks and hurling a variety of objects around the house. Additionally, the Irvings soon discovered that no secrets could be kept from Gef and he even seemed to be able to hear their words when they whispered. He was fond of hitching a lift on the bus to

Peel and then spying on the bus depot workers, eaves-dropping upon their conversations and, on one occasion, even stealing a bus conductor's packed lunch. Not only that, but he would supposedly visit the Irvings' neighbours in secret and report his findings back to the family.

To help him with his clandestine activities, Gef seemed to possess the ability to become invisible and change his shape. One time, James described how he saw a tiger in the countryside near Cashen's Gap:

> "Early in 1932, [...] I saw, to my surprise, a very large cat, striped like a tiger...I thought this is no ordinary cat, so I slipped a cartridge into my single-barrel gun...The cat was a little ahead of me, but easily within range, and it turned through an open gate way...into a grass field. I was there a few seconds behind, and fully expected to see the cat, but no cat could be seen, look as I liked...I detailed my experiences to my wife on her return that night, when Gef called out 'It was me you saw, Jim'."

When asked about his origins, Gef said that he was from India, and gave some interesting but slightly incongruous details: "I was born near Delhi, India, on June 7, 1852. I have been shot at by Indians. I am a marsh mongoose. When I was in India, I lived with a tall man who wore a green turban on his head. Then I lived with a deformed man, a hunchback." He insisted that he was brought to England "from Egypt by a man named Holland", but didn't say how he came to live on the Isle of Man.

Unsurprisingly, word of Gef's existence spread quickly around the Island. Soon the Manx papers heard of the bizarre animal and, being sceptical of the whole thing, named him the 'Dalby Spook' and printed satirical articles about him. But, Gef's fame wasn't limited to the Isle and, in time, Britain's national newspapers took up the story too, helping to make Gef something of 'an international sensation'.

Early in 1932, the year after Gef had first made himself known to the Irvings, a female correspondent informed psychic researcher Harry Price that an acquaintance of hers, James T. Irving, had discovered an animal in his house which, "after a little coaxing, had developed the power of speech". The letter went on to invite Price to visit the Isle of Man and see for himself, should he so desire. At the time, Price was unavailable, but sent a friend by the name of Captain James McDonald to investigate in his place. McDonald arrived at the Irving's farmhouse on the 26th of February. His report to Price still survives.

On the first day of his investigation, the Irvings showed McDonald around the house and pointed out the places that Gef liked to spend time. Of the mongoose, though, there was no sign all day, until a voice cried out "Who is that bloody man?" as the Captain was leaving to return to his accommodation. Later that evening, when Gef was alone with James he talked of his dislike for McDonald, saying "I've been looking at the man, and I don't like him. He does not believe in me. He is a doubter!" Despite Gef's displeasure, McDonald returned the following day.

During tea, a needle was thrown at him, bouncing off a teapot and prompting James to comment that Gef had the ability to toss objects about the place and did so regularly. Later, McDonald reported hearing "shrill screams and knockings all over the house" followed by a loud thud that seemed to come from Voirrey's room. Upon investigating, McDonald discovered that a chair that had been left on top of Gef's sanctum had been knocked off somehow, causing the bang. After that, nothing else happened of note and so a disappointed Margaret went upstairs to Voirrey's room in an attempt to talk Gef into showing himself. The captain overheard Gef's reply: "He's damned well not going to get to know *my* inferior complex." In response, McDonald called up the stairs imploringly,

"Won't you come down? I believe in you!" but the stubborn Gef would only answer with "No, I don't mean to stay long; I don't like you!"

Upon reading McDonald's report, Harry Price was interested enough to arrange a visit to Cashen's Gap himself. Along with Richard Lambert, the editor of the BBC magazine *The Listener*, Price arrived on the island on the 30th of July. Lambert's function would be to help document the goings-on at Cashen's Gap and provide a witness should any unusual phenomena occur.

As with Captain McDonald, James Irving gave Price and Lambert the tour of Gef's favourite places and, much to the family's chagrin, Gef once again refused to put in an appearance. A second visit on the next day yielded the same results. Price described the Irving family as "heartbroken" and Gef only resurfaced when the investigators had finally gone.

Four years later, Price published his findings in his book *The Haunting of Cashen's Gap: A Modern 'Miracle' Investigated*. In it, he wrote that "[Lambert and himself] had spent many pleasant hours under the hospitable roof of the Irving farmstead, but could not determine whether, in our role of investigators, we had taken part in a farce or a tragedy."

After Price and Lambert left the Isle of Man, James sent some of Gef's hair to Price who then had it analysed by Mr. F. Martin Duncan of the Zoological Society of London. A subsequent letter described Duncan's findings:

> "I can very definitely say that the specimen hairs never grew upon a mongoose, nor are they those of a rat, rabbit, hare, squirrel, or other rodent...I am inclined to think that these hairs have probably been taken from a longish-haired dog..."

These findings would be reinforced when Price returned to Cashen's Gap and took sample hairs from the

Irvings family's sheepdog, which turned out to be "absolutely identical with the alleged 'mongoose' hairs". More evidence to suggest that Gef wasn't as real as the Irvings insisted came when imprints that were supposedly of Gef's teeth and claws were also given to Price. Analysis by Reginald Pocock of the Natural History Museum revealed that these prints displayed "none of the folds and textures that would have been expected from a real animal's skin", and indeed, were unlike any possessed by an extant animal.

So, what was Gef? Could the creature have simply been an actual mongoose? Of course, being mainly from southern Eurasia and mainland Africa, the mongoose is not native to the British Isles, but it is interesting to note the coincidence that in 1912 the occupants of the nearby farm *Eary Cushlinn*, had introduced mongooses to help curb the rabbit population. But there were too many tales of unexplained feats to explain away Gef as an ordinary animal, like the time when a bus driver told a reporter that Gef had been inside his home somehow, and that because of this, James was able to list all the contents of the man's house, "even in rooms that cannot be seen from the outside". Furthermore, many visitors to Cashen's Gap would bear witness to objects being thrown and knocks, bangs and strange sounds emanating from all over the house—behaviour which would have been impossible for a simple animal to achieve.

Although Voirrey described the creature as "a nuisance" and maintained that she would be glad if he left them alone, Price (in private correspondence) seems to have thought that the whole phenomenon was a fabrication based upon Voirrey's personality and her loneliness. He described her as someone who "you would conclude is old for her years, isolated though those years have been from the ordinary rough and tumble of human experience". He deduced that Voirrey "must have passed a curious childhood, without playmates or friends, always in the company of her elderly parents, seeing life from their remote and limited angle". Price sympathised with her plight, asking "What more natural but that the adolescent fantasies of a young girl, when found to be attracting attention from visitors, pressmen and sightseers, might become imperceptibly enlarged into a permanent fantasy—in the unconscious hope that thereby might arise some occasion of release for loneliness?"

A journalist for the *Manchester Daily Post* went a step further in blaming Voirrey. He claimed to have heard Gef's voice first-hand and penned an article with the headline "Schoolgirl may have Powers of Ventriloquism". He suggested that the truth behind the mystery lay not with a 'man-weasel', but actually what he described as Voirrey's 'dual personality'. Supporting this theory is a statement by a childhood friend of the young girl's, Kathleen Green, who outlined in a 2001 interview with Manx Radio that Voirrey had indeed been something of a talented ventriloquist and able to convincingly throw her voice. However, *Fortean Times* writer Christopher Josiffe's invaluable research into the Gef story points out that the trick of throwing one's voice is just that: a trick—accomplished through the clever use of misdirection and therefore entirely beyond Voirrey. Besides, on at least two occasions Gef's voice was heard by investigators when Voirrey was visible elsewhere and far outside of earshot, such as outside.

Another motive for Gef's conjuration could have been money.

Cashen's Gap was by no means a successful farm and the Irvings had little in the way of income. Here, we can return to Josiffe's research for clarification: despite the family's unfortunate financial situation, James actually refused to sell a photograph of Gef to a national newspaper, his reason being that he did not wish to lose what he considered to be a "rare memento". An even greater sum was later declined when an American theatrical agent offered to buy Gef for the considerable sum of $50,000.

Unsurprisingly, some of the Irving's neighbours openly believed that Gef was an elaborate hoax perpetrated not just by Voirrey, but also by her mother Margaret and they stated as much in letters to Price, some of which remain in the Harry Price archives. They asserted that mother and daughter wanted to abandon their difficult existence and "They were attempting to frighten [James] into selling up and leaving." James himself recorded in his diary his own thoughts upon the possibility of Gef being a hoax, writing that he often spoke with the mongoose when he was certain that they were alone and that "It would have been very hard to maintain such a charade over a period of years, in the close confines of a small house, without ever being detected."

About forty years later, in 1970, a journalist managed to track down Voirrey Irving. Walter McGraw of *Fate* magazine interviewed her and quickly became convinced that she was telling the truth—that Gef really did exist and that he really did talk, despite "every emotional and financial motive for saying otherwise". In Voirrey's own words: "I wish it had never happened. If my mother and I had our way, we never would have told anybody about it, but Father was sort of wrapped up in it. It was such a wonderful phenomenon that he just had to tell people about it."

Indeed, Voirrey seemed to be embarrassed about the whole event and reluctant to have been reminded of it, "Gef was very detrimental to my life." she told McGraw, "We were snubbed. The other children used to call me 'The Spook'. We had to leave the Isle of Man, and I hope that no-one where I work now ever knows the story. Gef has even kept me from getting married. How could I ever tell a man's family what happened?"

When asked directly whether Gef was a hoax that she had directly orchestrated, Voirrey denied any fabrication, saying "I was shy...I still am...[Gef] made me meet people I didn't want to meet. Then they said I was 'mental' or a ventriloquist. Believe me, if I was that good I would jolly well be making money from it now!"

She added that she still did not know what kind of animal Gef had been and that she wished he had just left them alone.

Nandor Fodor, research officer for the International Institute for Psychical Research, stayed with the Irvings for a week. He too dismissed the idea of a fraud, finding the Irvings to be "sincere, frank and simple" people. Fodor saw nothing of Gef during his stay but concluded after interviewing witnesses that Gef existed and could indeed talk.

Fodor proposed the idea that Gef was "A split-off part of James Irving's personality, a compensatory factor to the thwarted ambition and 'mental starvation' to which Irving's lonely life at Doarlish Cashen had doomed him." He explained further:

> "As a commercial traveller, originally, [James] horizons were too wide, both physically and mentally, to reconcile himself to the cabined and confined life of a sheep and goat farmer in a God-forsaken spot where he was constantly struggling against physical starvation. The problem of mental starvation, for a man of Irving's intelligence, must have been even more serious. There was no way to relieve it by conscious means. So his unconscious took care of the job and produced the strange hybrid of Gef, fitting no category of humans, animals or ghosts, yet having common features with all of them. Had Irving been a student of psychical research, the development of Gef would have proceeded, I believe, on more occult lines."

A similar conclusion was drawn by Christopher Josiffe: "Gef's fate seems to have been tied up in some way with that of James Irving's, the onset of whose illness coincided roughly with Gef's disappearance." He goes on to give this passage from a letter that James wrote to Captain Dennis (another man Price sent to investigate Cashen's Gap):

> "In the early days, 1931–1932, Gef would suddenly cease talking (late at night) and say, in what I would describe as a pleading and pathetic voice, 'Oh let me go Jim. Let me go.' as if I were detaining him by some power or force, other than physical. I asked where he wanted to go, and he always answered, 'I must go back to the under ground...' I said, 'Well, be off; I'm not keeping you.' He would then call out 'vanished' in a long drawn out manner, and he could be heard to jump either up or down...and there would be silence afterwards..."

Interestingly, no phenomena as intense as had originally taken place occurred after James' death in 1945.

Despite the large amount of public scrutiny, there is still no widespread agreement as to whether Gef was an exceptionally well-executed hoax, a poltergeist, a cryptid or something that defies nomenclature entirely.

After James died, Margaret and Voirrey left Cashen's Gap behind and moved to the mainland in 1945. It seems that Gef made no attempt to follow them. Leslie Graham, the farmhouse's new owner, reported nothing out of the ordinary during his occupancy, although once he did trap a "strange-looking animal that seemed to be neither ferret, stoat nor weasel". After Graham too left Cashen's Gap the farmhouse stood empty and was eventually demolished for reasons unknown. Voirrey Irving died in 2005.

Whether he was real or not, Gef's name is still summoned up by the island's inhabitants, particularly when something goes missing.

It is unlikely that we will ever know the truth behind

Gef the Talking Mongoose, and so perhaps it is fitting to end this chapter with Gef's own words:

"But thou wilt never get to know what I am..."

9
The Zombie of Glydwish Wood

"In that evil wood everything is evil..."

Nestling amid the beautiful countryside of the Sussex Weald is a small village called Burwash. Here, listed buildings flank the neat, meandering high street and rows of deciduous trees lead the visitor east to the 11th century Church of St Bartholomew. A quaint and pleasant slice of English village life, to be sure.

However, behind the charming scenery lurks a dark legend concerning the woods that lie a little to the south. It is a story that tells of the tragic demise of a man who would be fated to return from the grave to split the stillness of the East Sussex countryside with the horrific wailing of a soul tormented.

The ghastly phantom that supposedly stalks through the aged trees of Glydwish Wood is believed to be that of David Leaney (or perhaps 'Leary' or 'Leany'), a 19-year-old farm labourer who, despite insisting that he was innocent of the crime of murder, was executed in 1825 by hanging.

Burwash was long a haven for smugglers. Many of the local populace sympathised with these roguish traffickers even to the extent of allowing skulls and crossbones to be carved unabashedly into their gravestones. Much continental contraband was brought up from the south coast of England, eventually to end up on the streets of London and other major cities in the South. And it was probably participation in this nefarious activity that saw both Leaney and a man named Benjamin Russel (at whose house in Burwash Leaney was a lodger) venture into the nearby Glydwish Wood at the dead of night.

Some say that the night's ambition was poaching or the stealing of corn, but, whatever the reason, illegality was certainly the intent. Fate, however, would see their scheme unravel grimly before its conclusion.

Sometime during the night, while endeavouring to return to their home, Russel suddenly grasped at his chest, collapsed and died of a heart attack right there in the woods—his ailment no doubt exacerbated by the weight of their contraband or the thought of reprisals if the two men were caught red-handed. Leaney, fearing prosecution for the night's deeds left Russel where he had expired and fled to his lodgings with the intention of returning the next day and orchestrating a 'surprised' discovery of his now deceased landlord.

But alas, Leaney's plan would not play out as he intended. Village gossip travelled quickly, and it suggested that Leaney and Russel's widow had been engaged in a romantic affair and that together they had hatched a murderous plot to bump off Russel with a dose of arsenic, and afterwards to claim to have found him dead of natural causes in Glydwish Wood. The hearsay was strong enough to prompt the local doctor, an old and blundering practitioner, to pronounce the cause of death as arsenic poisoning, perhaps even without having made a thorough examination of the dead man's body.

Despite their desperate protestations of innocence, Mrs. Russel was soon imprisoned and the wretched Leaney was sentenced to hang.

As the rough hemp of the executioner's noose slipped around his neck, Leaney swore to the chaplain that he would return from whatever realm death held for him and haunt those who he believed had brought him to this sad demise: "I beg of you believe me when I say I'm not guilty, and to prove it I shall return to haunt those people who have hounded me to my death." But this final claim of innocence went unheeded and Leaney was hanged.

Soon after the execution it was discovered, presumably by a more able coroner than the previous medic, that Russel had indeed died of a heart attack and that there was not a trace of arsenic in his corpse at all. Mrs. Russel was immediately released but, of course, it was too late for Leaney and it is thought by some that the wrongly-condemned man's spirit made true upon his final dark promise and even now stumbles through Glydwish Wood "in the form of a decomposing, ragged ghost, clutching at his throat [and] creating terror as he blunders through the woods".

In more recent times, Burwash gained fame as the beloved home of the celebrated author Rudyard Kipling, who lived at Bateman's (a splendid Jacobean house that lies near to the village) from 1902 until his death some thirty years later. Kipling took a great interest in the surrounding area and even penned *A Smuggler's Song* in recognition of the area's association with goods trafficking:

> *"Five and twenty ponies,*
> *Trotting through the dark,*
> *Brandy for the Parson,*
> *'Baccy for the Clerk,*
> *Laces for a lady, letters for a spy,*
> *And watch the wall, my darling, whilst the Gentlemen go by."*

It was not only the nocturnal deeds of the smugglers that interested Kipling; indeed, he became increasingly fascinated by all things supernatural as he approached his autumnal years. His biographer, Robert Thurston Hopkins, wrote that Kipling felt that "The dowland surrounding his home was full of pure magic and that the small area of woodland known as Glydwish Wood was particularly evil."

One night, a ghost hunt including Kipling and Thurston Hopkins was organised to explore the wood. Bravely, one of the participants endeavoured to venture away from the rest of the party. Suddenly, he found himself confronted by what was described as a repugnant, deathly apparition of a man, whose flesh was half-putrefied and whose hands clutched desperately at his own throat. A frightful apparition, no doubt—could this have been poor David Leaney's ghost?

It is very difficult to uncover eyewitness reports of the apparition itself. The excellent Anthony D. Hippisley Coxe writes in his 1975 book *Haunted Britain*:

> "The description of the ghost which [Robert Thurston Hopkins'] friend met in Gladwish Wood, the ragged thing that plucked at its neck, coughed and choked and moaned, is one of the most frightening passages I've ever read."

Kipling himself described the area as being "full of a sense of ancient ferocity and evil". Indeed, according to Peter Underwood, Kipling had quite a bit to say about the wood:

> "I have sometimes, while taking an evening walk through it, felt a secretive and menacing feeling all around me, holding me expectant and always on guard. In that evil wood everything is evil. There's a horrible suggestion of intelligence. It's not as though the woods were lonely or anything.
>
> "It's not empty—there's too much life there: a kind of ill-natured and venomous life. There is a spirit of some kind there, for one evening something suddenly gripped me

and despite my attempts to walk forward I was gradually forced back. I felt some unseen, unknown power pushing against me and in the end I was compelled to turn around and leave the wood."

It is not known when the last sighting of poor, ragged Leaney's apparition was seen. Perhaps his soul has finally found peace, or perhaps it is silently gathering energy, waiting to ambush the next foolhardy visitor with its terrible countenance.

Kipling himself is said to remain in spirit at Bateman's, lingering after death because of the tragic circumstances of his son's demise during the Battle of Loos in the Great War of 1914-1918. After the Battle, Jack was reported as missing, believed dead, aged only eighteen. Kipling never fully recovered from the death of his only son and suffered from depression for many years after.

Alas, Glydwish Wood is now said to be "sadly all but disappeared".

10
The Mystery of the Devil's Hoof-Prints

Did the Prince of Darkness really enjoy a brief holiday in 19th century Devon?

Eighteen fifty-five was a cold, bitter year. Temperatures dropped to cruel values and unemployment and hunger were rife. People all across Europe shivered and drew their blankets tightly around them. But, in spite of these subarctic conditions, one corner of England was warmed by what some insist was a bizarre visit from that master of hellfire himself—the Devil.

On the night of February the 8th, a slim covering of snow had turned England's south coast a perfect white. By midnight in the county of Devon, the snowfall had stopped and the quiet veil of night had settled upon the frozen land. However, for many of the county's slumbering citizens, it would be the last peaceful night they'd enjoy for some time.

Waking up to a morning that seemed like any other, people soon began to discover strange tracks that stretched across the landscape's virgin snow. For many miles the tracks continued, mostly following a straight path with almost unerring regularity. What's more, they seemed to have been branded into the snow somehow, not merely compressing it as normal footfalls tend to do, but melting it away until the green grass below was revealed.

Stranger still, they were in the shape of hooves.

As the hoof-prints continued, so did the peculiarities. The prints were found within a garden that was surrounded by a twelve-foot-high wall; underneath thick, snow-laden bushes and even seen entering a wooden shed only to come out through a squat hole in one of the shed's walls. They crossed a two-mile section of the River Exe, ending on one bank, only to begin again on the other. Through farmhouses and cottages and over high brick walls, haystacks and meadows the tracks persevered, only rarely breaking their regular gait. They were even reported to have walked across window sills, up drain pipes and onto high rooftops.

The prints were all over the place; far and wide. Some sources reported that they had covered ninety-six miles in a single night, from "Bicton in the east, Clyst St Mary in the north, across the Exe to Mamhead and Bishopsteignton and south as far as Barton, near Torquay."

In the town of Lympstone the hoof-prints approached every doorway before turning back on themselves and setting off away from the settlement.

Unsurprisingly, people all around the county looked at this otherworldly phenomenon with astonishment and fear. Reports from every parish confirmed that the prints were consistent in both dimensions and the length of the stride—and always hoof-shaped. Their placements also suggested that whoever—or whatever—made them was bipedal.

Men banded together to form search parties, arming themselves with guns, knives and whatever else was to hand. They followed the trails in attempts to discover the culprit, but the tracks had set the community on edge and paranoia and anxiety was rife. A slow-witted boy named 'Daft Danny' was nearly beaten to death when he was discovered by a search party dressed from head-to-toe in goose feathers. Men with hounds followed one trail to a forest which the howling dogs cowered at and steadfastly refused to enter. When the wintery sun dipped below the horizon and darkness fell across the land, the men roamed in bands with lanterns and torches. Rumours sprang up everywhere of alarming sightings of 'devil-like figures' prancing about the county. But, in spite of the ubiquity of the hoof prints and the many search parties that scoured the icy countryside, no sign of any creature that could have made the tracks was found.

In those days, news travelled at a far gentler pace than today—at a speed made even more leisurely by the less-than-perfect weather conditions, and so it wasn't until the next week that a local Saturday paper, *Woolmer's Exeter and Plymouth Gazette*, ran what was probably the first report about the hoof-prints. After that, the story was picked up by more of the country's newspapers and even competed with news reports coming back from the frontlines of the bloody Crimean War. From *The Times*:

> "Considerable sensation has been evoked in the towns of Topsham, Lympstone, Exmouth, Teignmouth, and Dawlish, in the south of Devon, in consequence of the discovery of a vast number of foot tracks of a most strange and mysterious description.
>
> "The superstitious go so far as to believe that they are the marks of Satan himself; and that great excitement has been produced among all classes may be judged from the fact that the subject has been descanted on from the pulpit."

The Times went on to describe the prints in some detail, saying that they were, "More like that of a biped than a quadruped, and the steps were generally eight inches in advance of each other. The impressions of the feet closely resembled that of a donkey's shoe, and measured from an-inch-and-a-half to two-and-a-half inches across." Others insisted that the prints were of a kind never before encountered and seemed to be accompanied by the "impression of the point of a stick" alongside them—undoubtedly thought to be the end of the Devil's trident.

Doors were barricaded at night and an epidemic of panic swept the god-fearing county. Writing later in that venerable tome, *Devon and Cornwall Notes and Queries*, Henrietta Fursdon described how her father, who was the Vicar of Dawlish at the time, was kept busy by his frightened flock:

> "The footprints occurred during the night, and since my father were a vicar he were immediately called for by curates, churchwardens and parishioners. Everyone wondered what he thought about the footprints that were all over Dawlish. They were made of a cloven hoof and were seen in a long row that seemed to never end. I remember it clearly how I, myself, saw the footprints and how I, like a child, were filled of fear for this unknown beast that roamed the place. But it wasn't just us children that were afraid: the servants refused to go out after nightfall, even if it were just to close the gates."

Some researchers claim that local clergymen took advantage of the community's hysteria and that it was they who first suggested that the Devil himself had been stalking the Devonshire countryside in his eternal search for sinful souls. These Hellish rumours travelled like wildfire.

While fishermen spoke of hoof-prints emerging from the sea at Teignmouth as though the biped to blame was somehow of aquatic origin, a host of other people came forward with their own explanations for the strange phenomenon. Many suggested animals were at the heart of the matter. Among them, roaming racoons, scurrying rats, waddling swans and jumping otters were all put forward. The renowned naturalist Sir Richard Owen received a sketch of the tracks and suggested that it was the humble badger that was the cause of the tumult. Badgers, Owen described, place their back paws in the tracks that are left by the front paws, therefore clearing up how the tracks in Devon's snow appeared to come from a two-legged creature. He explained that the strange, hoof-like shape of the prints was the result of 'freeze-thaw action'. Owen admitted in *The Times* that he had not examined the prints in person.

One of the more recent animal explanations comes from writer Mike Dash. In an article published in *Fortean Studies*, Dash suggested that some of the prints, including those found high upon rooftops, might have been made by hopping rodents such as wood mice. He argues that prints in the snow left by leaping mice resemble that of a hoof-print because of the way its limbs and body travel when it jumps.

The question of how experienced farmers and life-long country folk failed to recognise the tracks of such common animals as badgers and mice remains unanswered.

Bizarrely, the finger of blame was even pointed at kangaroos. In a letter to the magazine *Illustrated London News*, the amateur artist and vicar of Exmouth, Reverend George M. Musgrave, wrote:

> "In the course of a few days, a report was circulated that a couple of kangaroos escaped from a private menagerie (Mr. Fische's, I believe) at Sidmouth."

Of course, kangaroo tracks are most unhoof-like. Yet another explanation comes from thriller writer Geoffrey Household who suggested that "an experimental balloon", released unintentionally from a nearby dockyard, might have left alien marks in the snow for unwitting witnesses to stumble across and misinterpret. It seems that the balloon's mooring (or 'ballast') ropes had metal shackles on the ends and trailed behind it, dragging and 'hopping' along the ground. There certainly seems to be some truth to Household's theory as in early February 1855 a high-altitude observation balloon was in place at the Devonport Dockyard. As a snowstorm approached the coast, the naval detachment in charge saw this as an opportune moment to test the balloon's capabilities in arctic conditions. Duly inflated and attached to a privately-owned boat via a steam winch, the balloon got into trouble from the outset. The high winds pounded it with such force that the boat itself was in danger of capsizing. The crew were forced to cut the balloon loose and it was blown away with its mooring ropes trailing behind.

Faced with the possibility of having to settle expensive compensation claims, the Admiralty kept the event away from the public. A certain Major Carter (Household's primary source) claimed that his grandfather had worked at the dockyard at the time of the incident and had told him that the whole story had been concealed because the balloon had destroyed conservatories, knocked over greenhouses and smashed windows before finally descending. Whether the balloon could have travelled in a zigzag pattern, visited the front doors of houses in Lympstone and somehow managed to elude being caught on trees and bushes is another matter.

The Devil aside, some explanations have reached levels of wild eccentricity with even that curious figure 'Spring-Heeled Jack' being held responsible (alongside visiting aliens with malfunctioning equipment). Even a plot by four-hundred Romany gypsies on horse-shoed stilts was proffered at one point.

There is, of course, a great deal of scepticism about just how much we can take as fact from the reports at the time. Some investigators are doubtful that the hoof-prints really extended for a hundred miles or so, maintaining that, in rural Devon, it would have been physically impossible to follow their complete route in a single day.

Another reason for suspicion, as Joe Nickell points out in his book, *Real Life X-Files: Investigating the Paranormal*, is that the eye-witness descriptions of the prints were different from person-to-person and not as regular and uniform as sources such as the newspapers claimed. Certainly, it wouldn't be the first (or last) time that national newspapers exaggerated or sensationalised stories to capture the imagination of their readership and sell more copies. Indeed, according to some researchers the story was enthusiastically and intentionally embroidered by the newspapers in order to make fun of the pastoral Devonians, where there was thought to be a "vast amount of ignorance and superstition which still lingers in the rural districts of the county".

Other investigators such as Theo Brown (in her book, *Devon Ghosts*), have noted that a combination of many factors was probably at the heart of the fervour. Brown also insisted that there was a lack of proper evidence for the existence of a continuous trail and that the hoof-prints were neither uniform in appearance nor single file in pattern, going on to state that the prints were, "laid over several days rather than six hours," and adding that, "All the people concerned were quite content to leave the thing in the air, rather than spoil a good story."

Like Theo Brown, Mike Dash also deduced that the story was blown out of proportion by newspapers and Devonians alike and that the most startling reports appear to be "anonymous and second-hand". Tantalisingly though, Brown concludes: "To this day, no-one has offered an explanation which takes account of all the available evidence...even if the single-footed track only covered a part of the distance we still have no idea what creature could possibly have made it."

So, it seems likely then that an amalgam of many factors is behind the legend; a balloon trailing its ropes, hopping mice, blind fervour and a pinch of superstition. Add in exaggerated news reports and unreliable sources that contemporary and subsequent writers have taken as fact, and suddenly the recipe becomes one of inextricable mystery. Whatever the truth may be, the case of the Devil's Hoof-Prints remains a fascinating tale that is unlikely ever to be completely solved.

RECOMMENDED READING AND SOURCES

I include here a list of suggested reading material for those of you that are interested in furthering your knowledge of the endless legends and hauntings that lurk around the British Isles and other places. Some of the following publications and web sites have provided source material for this book.

Peter Underwood, *The A-Z of British Ghosts*, Chancellor Press, 1992.

Peter Underwood, *This Haunted Isle*, Brockhampton Press, 1998.

John and Anne Spencer, *The Ghost Handbook*, MacMillan, 1998.

Joe Nickell, *Real-Life X-Files: Investigating the Paranormal*, The University Press of Kentucky, 2001.

Richard Jones, *Haunted Britain and Ireland*, New Holland, 2001.

Richard Jones, *Haunted London*, New Holland, 2004.

Antony D. Hippisley Coxe, *Haunted Britain*, Pan Books, 1975.

Richard Holland, *Supernatural Clwyd*, Gwasg Carreg Gwalch, 1991.

Affleck Grey, *The Big Grey Man of Ben MacDhui*, Birlinn Ltd, 1994.

David Brandon and Alan Brooke, *Shadows in the Steam*, The History Press, 2009.

Jason Karl, *An Illustrated History of the Haunted World*, New Holland, 2007.

Michael Williams, *Supernatural Dartmoor*, Bossiney Books, 2003.

Theo Brown, *Devon Ghosts,* Jarrold Publishing, 1982.

Jan-Andrew Henderson, *The Ghost that Haunted Itself: The Story of the MacKenzie Poltergeist*, Mainstream Publishing, 2001.

Thomas Corum Caldas, *The Hangman, The Hound and Other*

Hauntings: a Gazetteer of Welsh Ghosts, Llygad Gwalch, 2010.

Dr Melvyn Willin, *Ghosts Caught on Film: Photographs of the Paranormal*, David & Charles Ltd, 2007.

John Fraser, *Ghost Hunting: A Survival Guide*, The History Press, 2010.

Harry Price and Richard Stanton Lambert, *The Haunting of Cashen's Gap: a Modern 'Miracle' Investigated*, Methuen & Co, 1936.

Nandor Fodor, *Between Two Worlds*, Parker Publishing Company, 1964.

James Wentworth Day, *The Queen Mother's Family Story*, Robert Hale Ltd, 1979.

Ghost Voices Magazine, bi-monthly [now discontinued], Dragoon Publishing.

WEB

www.MysteriousBritain.co.uk
www.Unexplained-Mysteries.com
www.ForteanTimes.com
www.BigGreyMan.co.uk
www.GhostClub.org.uk
www.UncannyUK.com
www.ParanormalDatabase.com
www.SPR.ac.uk (The Society for Psychical Research)
www.Unexplained-Mysteries.com/column (Mike Heffernan's column)
www.Haunted-London.com
www.DalbySpook.110mb.com (An excellent web site about Gef the mongoose)
www.MikeDash.com
www.FateMag.com

Chapters 2, 5, 9 first published in *Ghost Voices Magazine*. They appear here in an updated, rewritten form.

Many thanks to Lesley Symons for her extensive knowledge of Chambercombe Manor, Lisa Evans at *Ghost Voices Magazine*, Duncan Codd, Katy Forde, Doreen Stout at Glamis Castle, Black Hart Entertainment and the City of the Dead Tours in Edinburgh.

Eerie Britain

Eerie Britain 2

Ten More of Britain's Most Terrifying and
Peculiar Real-Life Stories

By MB Forde

Eerie Britain 2: Ten More of Britain's Most Terrifying and
Peculiar Real-Life Stories by MB Forde.
First published October 2012.

Ebook edition's ASIN: B0089E40TG
The moral right of MB Forde to be identified as the author of
this work has been asserted by him in accordance with the
Copyrights, Designs and Patents Act 1988.

Eerie Britain 2

For Mum & Dad

Eerie Britain 2

CONTENTS

Eerie Britain

A BRISK PREFACE

Of the many countries that ghosts and ghouls stalk, Britain stands as the one which is most often said to be the home of such things. And not idly is this spoken, as this small and ancient land has long been riddled with all manner of frightening folklore and terrifying tales.

With the crumbling castles, cob-webbed mansions and creaky old public houses that Britain possesses in large numbers perhaps it isn't surprising that a generous slice of them are said to have picked up a few non-corporeal non-paying guests over the centuries. In fact, in some places, the resident spooks are packed in as tight as sardines in a tin can. One poll claimed that Britain had over three times as many supernatural hotspots as elsewhere on the planet, with more than half of the top ten most haunted locations in the world being found within the shores of this specter'd isle.

Real hauntings—those that cannot currently be explained—are pretty rare. In reality, most of the cases we read about in books and see on television can be explicated by rational thinking, a bit of research and the application of sensible methods. But still, there remains that small amount of cases that continue to utterly baffle believers and boffins alike. And it is this mystifying fraction that can capture the imagination like nothing else.

No matter which way you look at them, ghosts are controversial. Long have the battle lines been manned by those who stand steadfast on either side of an argument that has raged for hundreds of years. Perhaps someday ghosts will be accepted as spiritual incarnations of the dead. Perhaps someday they will be entirely explained by science and the natural world. With the advent of new investigative techniques, equipment and research, this realm of shadows might one day be brought into the light.

Of course, to dismiss ghosts as not existing in any form is rather rash, and in many ways just as harmful as

c

believing without question. There have been far too many reports of encounters with strange apparitions or peculiar events to disregard them all as hoaxes or errors of judgement. Elliott O'Donnell, in his 1924 book *Ghosts, Helpful and Harmful,* asked "For how can we expect to know all there is to be known about another world and the Entities that inhabit it, when we know so little about this world and ourselves?"

For now, though, while no end to the standoff is in sight, we can at least enjoy delving into what is a truly fascinating subject.

As with the first book to carry the *Eerie Britain* title, this offering digs only lightly into the technical side of ghost hunting; instead, it is primarily concerned with telling the stories behind some of the most intriguing and interesting places of the British Isles. These are places whose stories have been whispered for hundreds, sometimes thousands, of years. Thanks to the age of many of these stories, and the fact that they have often been passed down orally, their veracity is at times difficult to prove. To be frank, *all* old ghost stories and legends are the products of hearsay and embellishments to some degree and the truth behind them can elude even the most tenacious of researchers, but that can also mean that the stories are more interesting, more...spooky.

The final pages of this book hold a recommended reading section. The titles and web sites found there either offer the reader a chance to further explore subject matters that have been merely touched upon in this book or are just worthy reads in their own rights. Many of them have been used as source material for this work.

Hauntings remain an intrinsic part of the paranormal world and, aside from being fascinating, they are very human. Death, fear, honour, revenge, hate and love: ghost stories bring to us all the facets of good drama often set against stunning backdrops and otherworldly mise-en-scène. Theatrics aside though, who doesn't like a nice headless horseman or a good, old-fashioned walled-up nun?

So, draw the curtains, cut yourself an extra large piece of that chocolate cake you've been saving for Aunt Maud (she doesn't deserve it anyway), throw another log onto the crackling fireplace and snuggle into the heavy folds of a fleecy onesie as we cast a glance at ten more of the most petrifying places, ghoulish goings-on and horrifying haunts to ever grace the British Isles.

How the graves give up their dead.
And how the night air hideous grows,
With shrieks!

-*The Feast of Blood*

1

The Berkeley Square Horror

Why did one of England's most sought-after post codes stand empty for so long?

"It seems that a Something or Other, very terrible indeed, haunts, or did haunt, a particular room. This unnamed Raw Head and Bloody Bones, or whatever it is, has been sufficiently awful to have caused the death, in convulsions, of at least two foolhardy persons who have dared to sleep in that chamber."

It was *the* ghost story of Victorian London. So notorious were the tales surrounding 50 Berkeley Square that sightseers in the capital would walk to Mayfair just for a glimpse of the infamous house—and perhaps with the hope of catching sight of the "Raw Head" or "Bloody Bones" that the author and artist Charles George Harper speculated in his 1907 book Haunted Houses might be behind the frightful goings on. And certainly, if the many grisly stories concerning Number 50 are true, then it is one of the most dangerously haunted houses in the world.

Or, at least it used to be.

The first notable occupant of 50 Berkeley Square was the Prime Minister George Canning. He moved in sometime around 1770 and spent time there until his death in 1827. Canning was known as a man of considerable confidence and wit—"a passionate, active, committed man who poured his energy into whatever he undertook," according to Rory Muir's *Britain and the Defeat of Napoleon*. His political career peaked with a time as Foreign Secretary and a short term as Prime Minister. Canning's total period in office remains the shortest of any Prime Minister of the UK, standing at a mere 119 days. When it comes to Number 50, it was Canning that might have been the first to make note of some kind of paranormal phenomena occuring at the house. Most writers on the subject tend to say that Canning heard strange noises and "experienced psychic phenomena" while living there, although reliable details that reveal more to us are hard to come by, meaning this all must be taken with a large pinch of salt.

After Canning's death, according to *The Pall Mall Magazine*, the house was leased by a woman called Miss Curzon. Details regarding her life are sketchy at best, with even her forename of Elizabeth at first proving elusive. She certainly made the most of Number 50, as she occupied it until she passed away in 1859 at the ripe old age of 90. Surviving is an interesting quote from one of Miss Curzon's employees, a Mr. George Vincent, who would go on to be Head Porter at Brasenose College, Oxford:

> "May I be allowed to say that I entered the house, 50, Berkeley Square, London, on March 20, 1851, in the service of the late Miss Curzon, who died in May, 1859? During the nine years I was in the house, and I have been in it at all hours alone, I saw no greater ghost than myself."

He would add, in a subsequent correspondence, that he

wasn't even aware of there being a sinister reputation surrounding the house. Despite Mr. Vincent's lack of ghostly encounters, it was during Miss Curzon's time at the house that it began to make a name for itself. By the early 1870s its infamy had certainly spread beyond Mayfair's boundaries, but it was not until a decade later that writers and journalists began to take greater notice. *Mayfair Magazine* wrote about the house many times. On the 10th of May, 1872, it published this intriguing insight into the growing legend:

> "The house in Berkeley Square contains at least one room of which the atmosphere is supernaturally fatal to body and mind. A girl saw, heard, and felt such horror in it that she went mad, and never recovered sanity enough to tell how or why. A gentleman, a disbeliever in ghosts, dared to sleep in it, and was found a corpse in the middle of the floor, after frantically ringing for help in vain. Rumour suggests other cases of the same kind, all ending in death, madness, or both, as the result of sleeping, or trying to sleep, in that room."

Not only that, but *Mayfair's* article goes on to tease us with the introduction of a most mysterious character:

> "The very party walls of the house, when touched are found saturated with electric horror. It is uninhabited save by an elderly man and woman who act as caretakers, but even they have no access to that room. This is kept locked, the key being in the hands of a mysterious and seemingly nameless person who comes to the house every six months, locks up the elderly couple in the basement, and then unlocks the room, and occupies

himself in it for hours."

Who this enigmatic chap was remains a mystery and he doesn't seem to crop up anywhere else.

After Miss Curzon's death the house was lived in (or owned) by Sir Charles Young, seemingly without ghostly intrusions of any kind. Following Sir Charles' occupancy, the house was supposedly well-known in the area as being empty. Local rumour must have put this vacancy down to the sinister reputation that surrounded it, and which, by this time, was widespread. Lord Lyttelton (presumably George Lyttelton, the fourth Baron Lyttelton), wrote to the long-running journal *Notes and Queries* in November 16th, 1872, regarding Number 50. He said: "It is quite true that there is a house in Berkeley Square (No. 50), said to be haunted, and long unoccupied on that account. There are strange stories about it, into which this deponent cannot enter."

Confusingly though, at this time it seemed that the house was occupied: by a man called Thomas Myers. Chris Gray of *The Independent* newspaper writes that the house was actually bought by Marcus Samuel, the First Viscount Bearsted. Samuel would later form the company Shell in 1897 and become the Lord Mayor of London for a brief time. It seemed that it was he who owned the property and rented it out to this Thomas Myers chap. Under Myers' control the house's dark reputation increased ten-fold.

Myers was what one writer called "an odd cross between Scrooge of *Christmas Carol* and Miss Havisham of *Great Expectations*", and this description seems not to be much of an exaggeration. Myers had leased the house for his fiancée and had even bought new furnishings to her taste, only to be jilted suddenly by his beloved wife-to-be. This rejection would deepen the mysterious reputation of Number 50, for Myers did not take the event well: "this disappointment is said to have broken his heart and turned his brain. He became morose and solitary, and would never allow a woman to come near him". Supposedly,

Myers became utterly reclusive and would lock himself in the house's top-most rooms, away from everyone he knew and a society that his paranoia spurred him into thinking mocked him behind his back. Only at night would he emerge and wander around the empty house with a lit candlestick in his hand. Slowly, inexorably, people conjectured that this living spectre of a man fell into madness.

Inevitably then, under Myers' occupancy Number 50 fell into a sorry state. He even failed to pay his taxes, and, after an application by the collector of taxes at Marlborough Street Police Court, a warrant for his arrest was issued. Even then, the reclusive Myers failed to appear in court. Bizarrely by today's standards, the magistrate excused his absence due to Number 50 being a well known haunted house, adding that "the house in question [...] has occasioned a good deal of speculation amongst the neighbours". He wasn't let off, though, and goods or property to match the cost of his debts were ordered to be seized.

When he died, Myers left his estate to one of his relatives, a woman recorded only as Miss Myers—it is possible that she was a younger sister. Like her benefactor, she was not in particularly good health and was confined to her bed. Consequently, she too neglected the house in Berkeley Square. In 1879, *Mayfair* published yet another article about the property, printing that the house was in a very poor state indeed:

> "With windows, caked and blackened by dust, full of silence and emptiness, and yet with no notice about it anywhere that it may be had for renting. This is known as the haunted house in Berkeley Square."

It seems that after Miss Myers' tenure, the Liberal Party politician named Lord FitzHardinge (Francis William FitzHardinge Berkeley, 2nd Baron FitzHardinge) leased the house to a man named Fish, who was, by all accounts, a well-known builder in the area. It is fair to assume that this Fish fellow fixed the place up and restored some, if not all, of its faded grandeur. Despite this, the stories about 50 Berkeley Square remained in the public's collective consciousness and even more outlandish ones began to circulate.

Again according to *Notes and Queries*, "the Berkeley Square mystery was, for a long time, matter of constant comment in society, but that of the thousands who believed in it not one was at the pains to knock at the door."

By now, the supernatural horrors of the house had been given a more specific home to better emanate from: a single mysterious room in the attic. This room became the hub around which many tales were based, with a variety of phenomena taking place or originating there.

One such story describes a man who moved into Number 50 with his two adolescent daughters. The girls took an instant dislike to the townhouse and remarked that its scent was redolent of "the animal cages at the zoo". A maid was sent upstairs to make ready a room for the arrival of a Captain Kentfield; the eldest girl's fiancé. Suddenly, blood-curdling screams shattered the quiet, and the house's occupants hastened to find the source. Upstairs, they found the maid. She had all but lost consciousness and was sprawled upon the floor. The family asked her what had happened to have laid her so low, but the only thing the girl would say was "Don't let it touch me, don't let it touch me!" She would never recover and died in a hospital bed on the following day.

Showing considerable bravery (or a generous helping of stupidity), Captain Kentfield decided to confront the legend and spend the next night alone in the notorious room. Seemingly untroubled by the fate of the maid and the myriad dark tales that surrounded the place, the confident Captain—grasping a candle in one hand and a pistol in the other—headed upstairs. In spite of his bravado, he would not last the night.

After a mere half hour, his screams—half-strangled by fear—were heard coming from the room. They were followed by the percussive crack of a single gunshot. Again the family rushed upstairs; but they were too late to help the man, for he was already stone dead, lying on the floor with his face twisted in petrified terror. The cause of death was said to be fright.

It's a gruesome tale for sure, but also one that has clearly been shaped by many a story-teller's hands. In fact, the idea that a young girl enters the room of horror, dies from fright and then is followed by a courageous young gentleman who, though armed, also expires in a similar manner has become something of a template for a number of stories about 50 Berkeley Square.

For example, another story concerns a chap by the name of Sir Robert Warboys and bears many telling similarities to the Captain Kentfield story. Warboys was a dashing young man, a notorious rake according to some, with a large family seat near Bracknell, Berkshire. In 1840, while in a public house in the Holborn area of London, the 20-year-old Warboys (he is 30 years old in other versions) sat listening to a discussion about the supernatural. Amongst his drinking partners were the Lord Cholmondley and a Mr. John Benson. It just so happened that Benson owned Number 50 at that time and, of course, the conversation turned to the horrors of that iniquitous upper room. Warboys stated brashly that he did not believe in the "unadulterated poppycock" of ghosts and goblins and to prove it he offered a wager: he would spend the night alone in the haunted room. A cool one hundred guineas were thrown into the kitty and the bet was sealed.

The following evening the friends gathered in Benson's house and Warboys prepared to go through with his promise. He carried a gun and a small bell that he could use to summon help if necessary. The story goes that, sometime after midnight, there was an almost inaudibly faint ring of the bell followed by a "ferocious peeling". As the friends ran up the stairs they heard the unmistakable report of a gunshot. They threw open the door to the haunted room.

There, lying supine on the bed, was Warboys; his lifeless face locked in an expression of sheer ashen dread. Like Kentfield and the maid, Warboys was pronounced to have been frightened to death.

There are many more stories that follow this Kentfield/Warboys template, each with minor variations of names and details. But whether they are true or not, they must have been believed by some contemporaries, for as a result of its grisly reputation, it seems that whoever owned Number 50 found it difficult to find tenants to occupy it. After Myer's death it appears to have remained empty for long periods. Well, empty of mortal inhabitants, anyway, for it was said that eldritch noises emanated from the interior on occasion; along with ear-splitting screams and the scraping and thudding of what sounded like a heavy body being dragged down a flight of stairs. Eerie lights would be seen drifting about the many rooms, observed by startled onlookers peering through the grimy windows from the street adjacent.

On a freezing cold Christmas Eve in 1887, two sailors from one of the Royal Navy's last small ironclads, HMS *Penelope*, were on shore-leave in London. Edward Blunden and Robert Martin had already blown what wages they had on alcohol, and now, as the winter wind whipped around them and chilled them to the bone, they were on the lookout for shelter. With no money to pay for lodgings, the two seamen decided to find an empty house to break into. They saw Number 50.

It was easy to gain entry. Inside was damp and a thick layer of dust coated everything; clearly the house had been empty for some time. Blunden and Martin found better conditions the further up they went, eventually stopping at the highest level—as luck would have it, in the haunted room. Unknowingly, they made themselves as comfortable as they could, shared some tobacco and a few words and then drifted off to sleep.

Suddenly, they were jolted back to wakefulness by loud noises nearby. It sounded as though a pair of heavy boots was ascending the main staircase. Without warning, and before the pair could react, the door to their room was thrown open and "a hideous, shapeless, oozing mass began to fill the room". Robert Thurston Hopkins described what happened next with a vivid account from his 1956 book *Cavalcade of Ghosts*:

> "They were out of the bed in a split second and dashed towards the window where they had left the only weapon they possessed, a rifle with which one of the sailors had propped open the window. The intruder took up a position, with large outspread claws, between the bed and the door, thus obstructing the way...
>
> "...It stood for a moment in a dark corner near the door, and the sailors could not see what manner of face the thing possessed—animal or human. But soon it began to move towards them...it crept, panted, shuffled across the room, making scratchy sounds on the bare boards which might have been the scraping of horny claws."

One of the sailors managed to dodge the thing and raced down through the darkened house. He sprinted desperately through the cold streets until he found a bobby on his beat. Upon relating his encounter, the policeman agreed to accompany him and the two returned to the house. Outside, a grisly sight was waiting for them.

Impaled upon the cast iron railings was the limp body of the sailor who had been left behind. He had chosen to jump out of the window to his certain death rather than face the "evil in the room above". Or perhaps he was pushed...

It's a fantastically macabre yarn. The earliest source for this sailor story seems to be the Irish author Elliott O'Donnell, and it is to the Berkeley Square section of his 1924 work, *Ghosts, Helpful and Harmful* that we turn now. In it, the story appears, although his version says it happened sometime in the 1870s, with 'Bert' and 'Charlie' being made up for the sailors' names instead of Edward Blunden and Robert Martin. O'Donnell, who described himself as "Britain's No.1 Ghost Hunter" on the front cover of his 1956 book, *Phantoms of the Night*, had several ideas for what the 'horror' of Berkeley Square might have been caused by. He supposed that "The ghost the two sailors saw was probably an elemental, possibly attracted to the house either by some crime or series of crimes committed in it or on its site; or else by a pool of water that once stood on the site (stagnant water, apparently, has a peculiar fascination for a certain species of elementals) or else, again, by the vicious thought and acts of some previous occupant."

For his own part, O'Donnell has been accused of making up the story of the two sailors entirely.

Despite the skeptics, even into the next century the house's reputation persisted, and it became a kind of macabre tourist attraction. Illustrating this is a passage from Charles Harper's *Haunted Houses* where he writes that "The haunted house in Berkeley Square was long one of those things that no country cousin come up from the provinces to London on sightseeing bent, ever willingly missed". Rudyard Kipling even used it as a location in his poem Tomlinson which was published in 1892. The first few lines give a flavour:

Now Tomlinson gave up the ghost at his house in Berkeley Square,
And a Spirit came to his bedside and gripped him by the hair—
A Spirit gripped him by the hair and carried him far away...

So just what was it that allegedly created such a fuss amongst Mayfairers and brought a terrible death to any person foolish enough to meddle with it?

Well, the 'thing' of Berkeley Square has been described in a variety of ways: "a man-ghost with an unbelievably ghastly face; a face white and flabby with a huge gaping mouth black as pitch", a formless mist, a gelatinous slime that slithered about and smelled foully, the evil ghost of that old recluse Mr. Myers, and even as "an animal creature with many legs and tentacles, a monstrous thing which looked liked it might have crawled from London's sewers". So it could be almost anything, really—as long as it's utterly hideous and fairly smelly.

Besides the main feature, other things went bump in the night at Number 50. Furniture moved by itself; according to one researcher, on occasion such furniture was actually thrown out of open windows onto the street below. Screams and moaning cries were heard by passersby, phantom bells rang out and strange figures were seen looking out of the darkened windows to the street below.

Writer Tom Slemen tells us that early in the year of 1937, a lady named Mary Balfour moved into an apartment in the nearby Charles Street. From her kitchen window she could see part of the buildings on Berkeley Square, including Number 50. One evening, she entered the kitchen to discover her maid statuesque, eyes transfixed on something out of the window. The maid pointed with a shaking finger, wordless, and Mary Balfour followed her gaze. In the rear of the house opposite, through a window, the two women could see the pale-faced apparition of a man dressed in an old-fashioned wig, light coat and breeches. Later, they related their sighting to a doctor who told them that the house was currently unoccupied except by workmen, but only then during daylight hours and that they must have seen one of 50 Berkeley Square's many ghosts.

The workmen themselves had also seen one of the house's apparitions. A little girl in a kilt had appeared to them on a section of the stairs and she had also been sighted in various parts of the upper floors. She was supposed to be a sad little thing, apparently killed by a cruel servant.

Another ghost to wander these rooms and corridors is known to some by the name Adeline. She was held captive by her lecherous uncle and died, falling from an upper window during an escape attempt. Others say it was suicide. Her spirit seems to linger in the infamous attic room and is one of those that is said to be 'so frightening as to be fatal'.

Today

Over the years, many theories have been put forward to account for all of these curious phenomena. One popular idea is that the rumours of strange and frightening things began when a man called Mr. Du Pré moved into the house with his violent, mad brother. The brother was uncontrollable and so ended up being locked in one of the attic rooms and fed through a grille. His cries of anguish and torment "could be distinctly heard in the neighbouring houses". Perhaps it was this that helped to kick off or compound the house's sinister reputation.

When this Mr. Du Pré occupied the house is unclear. In fact, quite a few of the stories surrounding the house feature personalities that are very hard to pin down. For instance, there seem to be no records of Sir Robert Warboys outside of stories connected to 50 Berkeley Square, and his supposed family seat in Bracknell doesn't seem to exist, either.

The ubiquitous ghost hunter Harry Price researched "the Berkeley Square bogeyman" during the 1920s. After much digging about, he claimed that, in the 1790s, a gang of criminals used the house as a headquarters for their money counterfeiting and 'coin-clipping' endeavours. Price thought that perhaps the criminals had invented the ghost stories to keep prying eyes away. He also learned that the house had stood empty for long periods at a time and suggested that if any paranormal cause was to blame it would likely have been a very active poltergeist. Of course, producing evidence for such a thing would be a Herculean task nowadays.

So then, was there any truth behind Number 50's gruesome stories at all? Certainly, for a long time it was well-known to be a notorious property by the Londoners who lived and worked around Mayfair and many must have thought the stories true. Also, if the house did indeed remain vacant for any considerable time it would surely be proof positive to some people that the house's infamy was driving people away—after all, it exists in one of the city's most expensive and desirable postcodes, an area that, according to Charles Dickens's *A Dictionary of London* from 1879, was, "Commonly known as, [...] from the society point of view, the crème de la crème of residential London."

So what was it that started tongues wagging in the first place? The insane brother locked away, that jilted and eccentric recluse Myers, rumours put about by criminal gangs, an unusually empty residence, speculation, idle gossip? The fact is that all of these could have added to the mystique of the house at some time or another, building the house's notoriety until it became known as the haunted house of Berkeley Square. This supposition then becomes presented as fact by subsequent writers who each pen their own versions. From Rhoda Broughton's 1868 piece *The Truth, the Whole Truth, and Nothing But the Truth*, which some have said started the rumours in the first place (although Broughton apparently said that her version was nothing to do with Berkeley Square, instead claiming that it originated in the countryside somewhere: "...and I clothed it in fictitious characters and transposed it to London, which I have since regretted, as so many people have thence assumed it must refer to the house in Berkeley Square."), to Harry Price, Elliott O'Donnell, Robert Thurston Hopkins and many, many modern day writers, lots of people have built their works on existing accounts, whether they were true or not.

The fact remains that there has not been any single first-hand witness to the disturbances which has been amply recorded.

So what of this notorious house today? Well, 50 Berkeley Square is certainly not abandoned and derelict. In fact, it has long been inhabited. Nowadays, it is the renowned antiquarian booksellers Maggs Bros. that calls the town house home. Almost every nook and cranny of it is filled with illuminated manuscripts, and rare and unusual correspondence—a staggering 120,000 books. In spite of the exceptional and precious contents, from the outside, Number 50 looks pretty much like any other Georgian town house in the nation's capital and thousands of people must walk past it each year oblivious to its once-held title of "the most haunted house in London", or the home of the "nameless horror". Maggs Bros. itself modestly describes the four-storey brick building as nothing more than "a pleasant town house in the heart of Mayfair".

New stories of ghosts still manage to crop up now and then, with tales of miscellaneous phantoms jumping out at the book company's employees, and even that Maggs Bros. makes it an integral part of its company policy that the last two people working at night must leave the building together for their mutual safety. There is also supposedly an old framed police notice on display warning that the top floor of the building is not to be used for any purpose whatsoever. Ed Maggs assures me that this is all very much nonsense. Furthermore, that framed notice? Well, it's an air raid warning leftover from the Second World War.

Whether any spirits did inhabit the house during its long history will probably never be known, but, even if the house is quiet of the undead today, to the paranormal researcher the ferocity and horror of the stories about 50 Berkeley Square are thoroughly fascinating, and quite unmatched. For this reason, to those in the know, there will always remain a dark nightingale amongst the centuries-old plane trees of Berkeley Square.

2
Wicked Whitby

Is this picturesque seaside town a gothic portal to the spirit world?

The North Yorkshire Moors is home to an ancient landscape, brimful of fascinating histories and intriguing folklore. This is a land where undulating moorland gives root to wind-bent trees, rocky cliffs jut jaggedly from Jurassic strata and clusters of oak, ash, birch and rowan offer quiet havens to wildlife of all kinds. Aelred, Abbot of Rievaulx Abbey from 1142 to 1167 said of the Moors: "Everywhere peace, everywhere serenity, and a marvelous freedom from the tumult of the world."

Venture out to the Moors' north eastern edge and you'll find one of the most enduring and mysterious places in Britain: Whitby—a place long considered a ghost hunter's paradise.

Whitby nestles between two cliffs, straddling the 28-mile-long River Esk as it empties into the cold North Sea. It is a strikingly pretty place, criss-crossed by cobbled lanes that meander between higgledy-piggledy rows of shops and red-roofed cottages.

The town has for many centuries been an attractive

prospect for those seeking a place to live and work, and it grew considerably during the Middle Ages thanks to the successes of its fishing and whaling industries. With the introduction of the railway in 1839 it then became a popular destination for Victorian tourists who would flock to the town during the summer months in search of fossils, restorative sea air and the town's famous and fashionable black jet.

As if Whitby wasn't already blessed with enough attractions, it is also home to a great many interesting ghost stories. A suitable place to begin is with the place's most imposing and sombre landmark: the Abbey.

The town's eastern skyline is capped by the skeletal ruins of its Abbey of St. Hilda. This Benedictine abbey is grade one listed and stands next to another venerable grade one building, St. Mary's Church. Together they dominate the east bank, the Haggerlythe, and are reached by climbing the town's famous Church Stairs, or '199 steps'—something of a trial of stamina for the less athletic visitor (although certainly worth the effort). It is interesting to note that mourners in days gone by would have to carry the deceased's coffin all the way up these stairs.

The Abbey dates from 657 AD and has had a rich and turbulent existence, hardly surprising then that it is supposed to be haunted. Its first abbess, Hilda, was a truly remarkable and wise figure whose efforts to spread Christianity and encourage education in the area led to some of the earliest Anglo Saxon poetry and literature. The Venerable Bede recorded much of the details of her life and said "All who knew her called her mother because of her outstanding devotion and grace." Even now, Hilda is inextricable from the ruins and her shroud-wrapped spirit is said to manifest at different points around the Abbey's grounds and—most famously—in one of the topmost windows, usually during the late morning hours. The excellent web site MysteriousBritain.co.uk sheds more light upon this phenomenon and lets us into the secret:

"Crowds from far and wide used to gather at the west

side of Whitby Churchyard, between 10.00 and 11.00 in the morning, where there was a clear view of the north side of the Abbey and the highest window. When the sun shone on the window it created an illusion of a woman's form wrapped in a shroud. This optical illusion was presumed to be the ghost of [the] Abbey's founder."

Rather more elegiac, though, is this poem from Robert Tate Gaskin (1909) which describes Hilda's ghost:

> Likewise the abbey now you see,
> I made, that you might think of me
> Also a window there I plac'd
> That you might see me as undress'd
> In morning gown and nightrail, there
> All day long fairly appear:
> At the west end of the church you'll see,
> Nine paces there in each degree;
> Yet if one foot you stir aside,
> My comely pressence is deny'd
> Now this is true what I have said
> So unto death my due I've paid.

Another ghost legend attached to Whitby Abbey is that of a young nun. She fell in love with a dashing young knight and broke her sacred vows of chastity. Subsequently caught, she was bricked up alive. The story goes that she screamed for days until eventually her body gave in and she died. People have long reported seeing her ghost on the stairs leading up from the dungeon, begging for release. In some versions of this story the nun is named Constance de Beverley and the knight Marmion, but this seems to be confused with Walter Scott's epic 1808 poem about the Battle of Flodden Field which features characters of the same names.

Lastly, at daybreak on Christmas morning, choral harmonies are sometimes heard coming from within an empty building near to the Abbey. Are these the spectral warblings of long-dead monks?

Bagdale Old Hall

Whitby boasts another very old building besides the Abbey. Bagdale Old Hall lies near Whitby's heart. It is a Tudor manor house that was built in 1516 for the wealthy Conyer family. Now a hotel that retains much of its original features, it was once owned by a rather colourful character named Captain Browne Bushell. He was a fascinating figure who came to a sticky end in 1651 beneath an executioner's axe. A naval officer under the employment of the King of Spain, Browne returned to England during the English Civil War and allied himself to the Parliamentarian forces for two years. Later, he switched to the Royalists' side, saying "I then deserted the Parliament, being heartily sorry that ever I drew my Sword for such Masters; And (truly) had I as many lives, as I have haires [sic] upon my head, I should freely and willingly adventure them all for my second Master the King."

Eventually, Browne was arrested by Cromwellian forces. He was taken to London and charged with "the betraying, surrendering and yielding up of the castle and town of Scarborough" to which he pleaded not guilty, and also with various charges of taking up arms against parliament. The court judged him guilty of treason, to be executed by beheading on Saturday, the 29th of March. On the scaffold at Tower Hill, he addressed the large crowd with what some have described as an attempt at theatrical flair:

> "Christian people, I am brought hither to die, and to pay the wages of Death, for which I am not in the least sory [sic]; but rather conceive it a great mercy from Heaven, that God hath been pleased to use this means, for bringing me so much the nearer and sooner unto him: Yet I desire that the world may take notice, and understand, the true cause and grounds of this untimely Death."

After giving some history of his involvement in the Civil War, he asked the executioner if the block and axe were the same that his "late Royal Master received the fatal blow from". The answer came: "Yes Sir, these are the same". This seemed to please Bushell and he made his way contentedly to the block. The executioner lopped off his head in a single skilful blow.

According to some, Bushell might still be lingering on at Bagdale Old Hall. If the tales about his ghost are to be believed, he manifests as a strange, ethereal shape that moves around the staircase and produces clattering footsteps that travel up and down its stairs. One report even stated that his headless torso has been seen silhouetted against a window.

Perhaps it is Bushell who is also behind the poltergeist activity at Bagdale, where pots and pans have been flung around the kitchen and lights switched on by themselves. Is this the reason why the building remained empty for a long time? Or was it because of the disembodied children's voices that have been heard, sometimes whispering, sometimes playing and sometimes crying?

The Lighthouses

Whitby's historic landmarks continue with its two harbour lighthouses. Standing proudly at the tips of the harbour's piers, the lighthouses have helped to guide mariners into port for over a hundred-and-fifty-years. Both are haunted.

Run by the Port of Whitby, the stone-built, 83-foot-tall west lighthouse is open to the public during the tourist-filled summer months and is still partly in use, displaying a green light when a boat is expected to come into the harbour. This lighthouse is frequented by the one-armed ghost of a local man who "tended the lights" and is thought to have keeled over one day on the stairs inside the lighthouse on the West Pier, soon expiring of a heart attack. Authors seem divided as to whether the man's arm was severed in life when he fell to his demise, or whether it was an old injury. Either way, he seems to want a similar fate to befall others, because he is supposed to lie on the stairs inside and occasionally try to trip up unsuspecting visitors.

The 1854 eastern lighthouse isn't open to the public. Not to be outdone by its taller cousin, it is also replete with its own phantom. One summer, two brothers were in competition for the affections of a beautiful young girl called Sylvia Swales. For whatever reason, she found it too difficult to choose between her two suitors so her father set them a challenge: a boat race, with the winner taking Sylvia's hand in marriage. The two boys set out with enthusiasm, but soon a large wave capsized their boats. Both were swept out to sea where they drowned. Their bodies were later washed up on the nearby shore of Saltwick Nab. Sylvia blamed herself and resolved never to marry. Her sad ghost frequents the eastern pier, forlornly staring out to sea.

The Bargheist Coach

Whitby has a third and a fourth lighthouse, too. Whitby High Light and the South Light near it were put up in 1858 behind the Abbey. Also in this area a potentially spectacular phenomenon manifests. Paul McDermott in his splendid *Whitby Ghost Book* tells us more with this sparkling passage:

> "On the night after a burial of a seaman in the graveyard, a great black funeral coach pulled by six coal-black horses would appear without warning, galloping down Green Lane, the narrow road which runs beside the Abbey. Lit by the light of blazing torches carried by two outriders dressed in all black, it was driven by a ghostly coachman whose features were hidden by a voluminous black velvet cloak.

"Careering furiously along the lane and ignoring all that lay in its path, the coach would enter the graveyard and suddenly shudder to a halt by the newly made grave of the dead seaman. The door creaked open and out would step a long procession of wraith-like mourners clothed in black, who paraded silently around the grave. After their third passage, the dead man was seen to rise from his grave, join the party of mourners, and both he and they returned to the waiting coach. The coach then galloped off, crashing wildly down the precipitous Church track (known as the donkey road), which descends the cliff from the churchyard wall to the street below.

"At the bottom it turned sharply right, into Henrietta Street all the time picking up speed. The gruesome coach continued to hurtle along the cobbled street, onto the adjoining steep cliff known as Haggerlythe, and leaping into the air it plunged over the cliff's edge and into the foaming sea below.

"Not for the seamen of Whitby were the land-bound graves on the East Cliff. The sea knew which souls belonged to her and sent 'The Bargheist Coach' to reclaim them."

The Bargheist Coach is not to be confused with that terrifying spectral hound that is whispered to appear in Whitby; the Barguest.

A definitive spelling for this canine is as hard to pin down as eyewitness reports, with various people having it as any of the following: Barghest, Bargeist, Bargtjest, Bo-guest, Bargheist, Barguist, Bargest or Barguest. Whatever the spelling, he is a fearsome black beast; a hound of Hell in fact, with incandescent eyes, huge teeth and razor-like claws. His hunting grounds were—or perhaps still are—

the nearby moors and Whitby's starry night-time lanes. The legend goes that anybody who is misfortunate enough to hear his bone-chilling howls is fated to soon die.

Interestingly, while this demon hound clearly has roots in superstition and folklore, there have been quite a few modern day sightings of a 'Beast of the Bay'. What has been described as a "black panther-like cat" has been spotted on many occasions over the best part of the last decade; once even with a cub. The *Whitby Gazette* reports it being seen fairly often, with the last sighting in July of 2010:

> "The first sighting of the infamous Beast of the Bay in more than a year was reported to the *Whitby Gazette* yesterday morning. Retired teacher, Annabel Smith (62), of Front Street, Grosmont, was having a drink with friends in the White House pub on Friday night when she caught sight of the beast.
>
> She watched it for a few minutes before going outside where another table of women confirmed they too had seen a mysterious big cat as it was getting dark at around 10pm. She said: "It wasn't walking like a dog. It was walking like a cat. My friend who was with me, Veronica Nelson, saw it too and said it was definitely a big cat. It was far too big to be a domestic cat. It was just skulking, going from the sea towards the road."

Luckily, the Beast of the Bay doesn't seem to possess glowing eyes or a predilection for announcing impending dooms...so far.

Dracula

Of course, to the majority of people, Whitby is most famously associated with Bram Stoker's *Dracula*. And with good cause, for even though Stoker already had plotlines sketched and characters outlined for his book before he visited Whitby, many aspects of the fishing port ended up influencing his writing in some way.

The author and his family enjoyed a three-week-long holiday here during the summer of 1890, arriving in late July. He spent a great deal of time in the town, talking with the old sailors and fishermen and researching in the library (now a modern bar), and so are large number of little details of Whitby life made it into his seminal book.

For example, Stoker had originally planned to bring his vampire to England via the southern port of Dover, but once he heard the story of the recent wrecking of a Russian schooner, he was inspired to change his plans and make little Whitby into the gateway for the dreaded Count Dracula. The schooner in question was called Dmitry and its wrecking took place only five years prior to Stoker's visit, so the event would have still been fresh in the locals' memories. The *Whitby Gazette* once more provides us with the stirring details, this time from the 31st of October, 1885:

> "A little later in the afternoon a schooner was descried to the south of the harbour, outside the rocks. Her position was one of great danger; for being evidently unable to beat off, there seemed nothing for it but to be driven among the huge breakers on the scar. Her commander was apparently a man well acquainted with his profession, for with consummate skill he steered his trim little craft before the wind, crossing the rocks by what is known as the 'sledway' and bringing her in a good position for the harbour mouth.

> "The piers and the cliffs were thronged with expectant people, and the lifeboat 'Harriot Forteath' was got ready for use in case the craft should miss the entrance to the

harbour and be driven on shore. When a few hundred yards from the piers she was knocked about considerably by the heavy seas, but on crossing the bar the sea calmed a little and she sailed into smooth water. A cheer broke from the spectators on the pier when they saw her in safety.

"Two pilots were in waiting, and at once gave instruction to those on board, but meanwhile the captain not realising the necessity of keeping on her steerage, allowed her to fall off and lowered sail, thus causing the vessel to swing towards the sand on the east side of the harbour. On seeing this danger the anchor was dropped, but they found no hold and she drifted into Collier's Hope and struck the ground. She purported to be the schooner 'Dmitry' of Narva, Russia, Captain Sikki, with a crew of seven hands, ballasted with silver sand. During the night of Saturday the men worked incessantly upon her that her masts went by the board and on Sunday morning, she lay high and dry a broken and complete wreck, firmly embedded in the sand."

So, the real-life 'Dmitry' out of 'Narva' was transformed into the 'Demeter' out of 'Varna' and became the unfortunate ship that ferried Dracula to England's shores. The fearsome dog legend of the Barguest, recounted above, might have provided an idea too, as the vampire count assumed the form of a beast similar to the Barguest when he first arrived in Whitby, jumping from the stricken ship. Stoker also took inspiration from the now weather-beaten and jauntily-angled tombstones in St. Mary's Churchyard, with some of the epitaphs recorded in ten pages of his notes and providing character names, both major and minor (such as John Steward which became

Jack Seward).

Even the very name of Dracula was discovered in the old library where Stoker found William Wilkinson's verbosely titled *An Account of the Principalities of Wallachia and Moldavia with various Political Observations Relating to Them.* While browsing its pages, a passage caught Stoker's eye:

> "[In] the year 1444; when Ladislas King of Hungary, preparing to make war against the Turks, and engaged the Voivode Dracula* to form an alliance with him."

And the accompanying footnote:

> "*Dracula in the Wallachian language means Devil. The Wallachians were, at that time, as they are at present, used to give this as a surname to any person who rendered himself conspicuous either by courage, cruel actions, or cunning."

From then on, the iconic character that had before been named Count Wampyr now became Count Dracula.

The Dracula that William Wilkinson wrote about was, of course, Vlad III, Prince of Wallachia, and the Dracula epithet meant 'son of the dragon' rather than 'devil' (Vlad Tepes' father was named Vlad II Dracul of the Order of the Dragon). Vlad III would be given another nickname during his lifetime: Vlad Tepes—or Vlad the Impaler in English—for his habit of, well, impaling people.

Visitors to the town are given the chance to sit in the author's shadow on the Bram Stoker Memorial Seat that was put up in 1980 on a spot at the southern end of the West Cliff where he is supposed to have sought repose during his stay.

A Handful More
Even clothing in Whitby can take on an otherworldly aspect, for there's a tale about a haunted shawl of all things. This shawl was a fine item, made of expensive silk.

It had been taken from a woman by a pirate shortly before he murdered her. The dastardly pirate gave the shawl to his wife only for the dead woman to start appearing behind her whenever she looked in the mirror. The pirate's wife is said to have been driven mad by this and later died.

Whitby's strange and spooky stories don't stop there: there's Hob, a short, hairy and ill-tempered elemental spirit of some kind that deflates car tyres, "makes motorists skid and changes signposts around"; according to Anthony D. Hippisley Coxe in *Haunted Britain*, there's a decapitated phantom that wanders along a route between Prospect Hill and Ruswarp with its head under its arm; and a ghost called Goosey who haunts somewhere between Sleights and Ruswarp (quite a large area). Goosey, "a simple fellow", once was challenged to eat a whole goose in a single sitting. He won and thus earned his moniker. He was later murdered. Whether the crime was related to the challenge is unclear—in fact, most details about Goosey are unclear.

In the 1950s, a dark figure passed through the body of a startled railway worker, and earlier in that century, the headless phantom of a dead soldier appeared in front of his own family. Interestingly, alongside the Bargeist Coach, there is a second spectral coach and horses that is said to haunt Whitby's cobbled streets. This one rattles to a stop outside the Mission to Seamen before driving off towards an unknown destination. Finally, a strange, intangible mist has been sighted drifting down the West Cliff. Nobody knows what it could have been.

What is utterly tangible is the 'Hand of Glory' in Whitby Museum—perhaps a little too tangible for some people. For the Hand is exactly that: a real human hand, severed at the wrist.

The legends say that a Hand of Glory must come from a hanged man—an executed criminal—and its lifeless fingers bent to grip a candle made from the fat of the same man. In some places, the hair of the man was thought to be necessary to form the wick. The candle was then lit and would do several things for the bearer: send those around it into a deep slumber, unlock any doors that might bar entry to the holder of the Hand and, of course, light the way: an excellent tool for would-be burglars.

Whitby's Hand of Glory is a mummified example where the fingers are not coiled around a candle, but outstretched with the idea that the fingers would be lit instead of a central candle. It is thought to be the only one of its kind in existence and was found walled up in an old cottage in Castleton. It was then donated to the Museum in 1835. To illustrate an example of the Hand's use, the Museum offers this story, first published in Edwin Sidney Hartland's *English Fairy and Folk Tales*.

"One dark night, when all was shut up, there came a tap at the door of a lone inn in the middle of a barren moor. The door was opened, and there stood without, shivering and shaking, a poor beggar, his rags soaked with rain, and his hands white with cold. He asked piteously for a lodging, and it was cheerfully granted him; there was not a spare bed in the house, but he could lie on the mat before the kitchen fire, and welcome.

"So this was settled, and everyone in the house went to bed except the cook, who from the back kitchen could see into the large room through a pane of glass let into the door. She watched the beggar, and saw him, as soon as he was left alone, draw himself up from the floor, seat himself at the table, extract from his pocket a brown withered human hand, and set it upright in the candlestick. He then anointed the fingers, and applying a match to them, they began to flame. Filled with horror, the cook rushed up the back stairs, and endeavoured to arouse her master and the men of the house. But all was in vain—they slept a charmed sleep; so in despair she hastened down again, and placed herself at her post of observation.

"She saw the fingers of the hand flaming, but the thumb remained unlighted, because one inmate of the house was awake. The beggar was busy collecting the valuables around him into a large sack, and having taken all he cared for in the large room, he entered another. On this the woman ran in, and, seizing the light, tried to extinguish the flames. But this was not so easy. She poured the dregs of a beer jug over them, but they blazed up the brighter. As a last resource, she caught up a jug of milk, and dashed it over the four lambent flames, and they died out at once. Uttering a loud cry, she rushed to the door of the apartment the beggar had entered, and locked it. The whole family was aroused, and the thief easily secured and hanged."

While some of Whitby's many tales must be taken cum grano salis, the town is undeniably rich in folklore almost to a degree beyond compare, and it unquestionably deserves its high status amongst the country's most macabre and mysterious sites.

3

Ghosts and Murder at Samlesbury Hall

Indelible bloodstains and tragic love.

Settled amid leafy boughs, a short distance from the meandering waters of Lancashire's River Ribble (itself supposedly haunted by the water spirit, Peg O'Nell), Samlesbury Hall stands as a reminder of England's turbulent past. Now, the Hall's striking black oak and white quatrefoils stand in mute witness to far more peaceable goings-on; but it wasn't always so, for Samlesbury Hall's long history is one scattered with unrequited love, religious persecution and premeditated murder.

A dwelling of some kind has been on this site since at least the early 1300s and large sections of the existing hall date back to the 1400s when the site was the residence of the notable Southworth family. The Southworths prospered for many years, winning favour thanks to successful military service under various kings of England and displaying their martial prowess at such great battles as Agincourt and Harfleur. But their happy days were destined to fall by the wayside when the protestant monarch Queen Elizabeth I assumed the throne in 1558.

Being staunch Catholics, the Southworths refused to abandon their faith and so it became that many years of discomfort and hardship were ushered in. Like other families of the time, they endeavoured to keep their faith a clandestine affair, with secret Masses taking place in the seclusion of the surrounding woods. At least three priest holes were added to the Hall's interior in various places.

These tiny hidden chambers were built by the diminutive Jesuit lay brother Nicholas Owen. Owen found a degree of fame as the rather ingenious engineer behind thirty years' worth of priest holes. Despite being always careful to take as many precautions as he could, such as working alone and usually at night, he himself was arrested in early 1606, giving himself up after four days without food or water in one of his own cramped constructions. Later that year he was taken to the Tower of London and died under gruesome torture. In spite of what he had to endure, Owen never gave his interrogators any information and he was made a saint in 1970 by Pope Paul VI. So good was his work at concealing priest holes that even today it is thought many of his creations remain undetected.

At Samlesbury Hall, however, at least one unfortunate fellow would not be saved by Owen's ingenuity. Sometime in the 1500s a priest was followed to the Hall by government soldiers and promptly discovered despite being secreted away in one of the building's priest holes. He was dragged out of his hiding place and summarily beheaded.

Legend has it that the ill-fated priest's blood stained the floor of his small room so intensely that nobody was able to wash it away—no matter how hard it was scrubbed. To hide the indelible stain, the room was bricked up for approximately two hundred years. It was eventually reopened in 1898. Even then, servants refused to remain in the house until the floorboards were replaced. To this day, the blood stain is said to occasionally reappear...

As grisly as the priest's end may have been, and as

enduring the legend of the indelible bloodstain is, there is another Samlesbury spectre that enjoys far more infamy: the lady in white. Thought to be Lady Dorothy (or perhaps Dorothea) Southworth, her tale is one of youthful romance and terrible tragedy.

Lady Dorothy fell in love with a dashing young local man from the de Hoghton family. Unfortunately for the two lovers, the de Hoghtons were as strongly Protestant as the Southworths were Catholic and neither house wished a union with the other. Consequently, Dorothy and her young beau were categorically refused permission to marry. Defying their families, the lovers continued to see each other in secret, meeting along the River Ribble's winding banks or amid the shade of the nearby woods. It was there in the woods that they concocted a daring plan to elope together. They hoped that once they were married their families would be forced to respect their sacred vows and their love for one another would be allowed to flourish. Alas, their hopeful (or naïve) arrangement was never to come to fruition for the scheme was overheard and the tale relayed back to Samlesbury Hall.

On the night of the planned elopement, Dorothy's brother waited in ambush for the rendezvous to take place. As soon as young de Hoghton arrived, Dorothy's brother sprang forth from his hiding place and killed him on the spot—not even sparing the lives of the young man's two retainers. The trio of corpses were hastily buried under the cover of darkness within the grounds of the Hall's chapel.

Adding to her misery, Dorothy had witnessed her lover's sudden and violent death. Local legend says that she was utterly inconsolable and had to be sent to a convent overseas where she descended further into grief-fuelled madness. Dorothy would later die at the convent, "the name of her murdered lover ever on her lips". A second version has her throwing herself from a high window to her death.

A variety of sources state that three sets of skeletal remains were discovered nearby to the Hall in the late

1800s when a "land drain or road works necessitated excavation". Could these have been the remnants of the luckless trio slain by Dorothy's ruthless brother? Some people certainly think so.

Popular legend has it that Lady Dorothy's spirit lingers on at Samlesbury Hall, tethered to the grounds where she grew up by the intense nature of her torment. For centuries there have been reports of a 'white lady' weeping and wailing, and walking solemnly through the grounds until she meets a "young knight" positioned in that most romantic of poses: upon bended knee. They walk together for short while and then face each other, entering into a heartfelt embrace, "then the forms rise slowly from the east and melt away into the clear blue of the surrounding sky."

Many witnesses have claimed to have had encounters with just such an ethereal white lady that flits across the estate on clear nights, floats down one of the Hall's many corridors, sobbing gently for her lost love, or is felt as a strange presence upon the creaking main staircase. Indeed, so often has the white lady been encountered that she has garnered widespread infamy as a very old and life-like apparition.

But perhaps there is a more rational explanation to the origin of the white lady's story. The popular website MysteryMag.com suggests that concealment of Samlesbury Hall's Catholic connections might have been behind Dorothy's ghost:

> "The Hall contained many items of papistry, which were eventually discovered by the authorities in 1592. So it was about the time Dorothy died that there was, perhaps, a 'need' for a ghost in the Hall and its grounds, to deter prying eyes. It may be then that the ghost story first emerged."

While this idea does give us an interesting angle upon

the legend's origin it doesn't explain away the myriad sightings of the white lady in the years since. Indeed, even in our modern age of silicon and cynicism there have been countless reports—"A long list of eyewitnesses"—of motorists and bus drivers seeing, meeting (and even stopping to pick up) the white lady while they travelled down the busy A59 road that passes close to the Hall...only for her to vanish into thin air. According to the television show *Great British Ghosts*, the apparition has been the cause of such fuss in the past that it even has a police record.

While the real story behind this particular haunting and its origin continues to be lost in the shadows of time, Samlesbury Hall remains a beautiful and much-loved property and, as such, this grade one listed building hosts many events, attracting thousands of visitors each year.

4
Dunwich Drowned

Spectres of a sunken city.

If you look out to sea from atop Dunwich's wind-battered cliffs you'll be greeted by a seascape much like any other around the jagged edges of the Britain Isles. But here, amidst the wheeling seagulls and hardy gorse, not all is as it first appears: for, hidden from sight beneath the cold waves of the North Sea, about half a mile out, there rests what used to be an entire city.

Taken from the land over hundreds of years by Nature's indomitable forces, this undersea settlement is known as Dunwich and was at one time a thriving and important location—the capital of East Anglia and the seat of its kings, no less.

The Romans used it as a trading port thanks to the deep anchorage offered by its harbour. Sadly, now almost all of the original Dunwich lies underwater and what remains habitable barely comprises a village. With a ravaged history such as this it seems quite fitting that the coastline here is said to embrace many a mystery, phantom and legend.

In the year 1086, Dunwich was a fast-growing hub with

a population of approximately three thousand people. It was recorded in the Domesday Book as being one of the ten largest settlements in the country, having at least six parish churches dotted around its neighbourhoods—it even boasted a Knights Templar church at one point. Its port guaranteed its status as a busy centre for trade, and people and goods of all kinds passed through its bustling markets. But then, sometime around 1286, disaster struck.

Massive, storm-whipped waves battered both Dunwich and the East Anglian coast that it clung to, and eventually a large portion of the helpless city was swept into the sea.

By the early 1300s, the port had recovered somewhat and was even then said by one source to be of a similar size to London; although this is perhaps something of an exaggeration. Despite its plucky resolve, Dunwich remained at the mercy of the sea and when more great storms hit in 1328 and 1347 another 600 houses and three churches from the lowest areas of the city were also lost to the briny depths. After that, further bad weather, flooding and coastal erosion reduced the settlement's size and population even more, until by 1602 it was a mere quarter of its original extent. By the mid-1800s, Dunwich was a "decayed and disfranchised borough", with the population standing at a much reduced figure: just 237 inhabitants.

Today, only a few relics of the old Dunwich still stand: the dwindling remains of Greyfriars, a 13th century Franciscan priory; and the Chapel of St. James which served the old leper hospital.

But what of the many legends and tales that surround this place? Well, conceivably the most infamous of Dunwich's supposed paranormal phenomena are the tollings of long-lost church bells. Said to happen most of all in December—when the sea is particularly tossed by frigid winter storms—local legend has for many decades insisted that the bells of the numerous sunken churches can still be heard echoing ominously across the waves. While this tale has become almost inseparable from Dunwich it is worth noting that the phenomenon is by no means unique to the area as legends of lost or sunken church bells tolling mournfully (and in spectral fashion) are to be found in quite a few places around Britain.

But for those who seek interesting stories, the bells are not all that Dunwich has to offer. For when the sun dips below the horizon the apparition of an Elizabethan sailor walks across the beach; seemingly wandering without aim, before turning to wade waist-deep in the sea and then clambering into a boat of some kind. After that, he vanishes. He has been seen by dog-walkers and fishermen alike, some of whom say he is searching hopelessly, endlessly for a lost lover. How this is known is unclear and more than likely a romantic later addition to the story.

The spectral sailor isn't the only one to spook the locals on this beach: the eerie sounds of laughing children have also been reported hereabouts. Of course, hearing this could either be heart-warming or utterly terrifying, depending on whether the children are laughing with playful delight, or something more sinister is afoot.

More love-based folklore appears in the form of *The Dark Heart of Dunwich*, a tale which comes to us from way back in the 1100s.

Despite being promised to a local man of means, Eva of Dunwich fell in love with a rather more rakish chap and the two ran off together. Sadly for Eva, her beau soon took advantage of her affections and then he promptly departed for adventures at sea—alone. Eva never quite recovered from the betrayal and one day she walked down to the beach, she cut out her own heart and tossed it into the foaming sea before her. Her spirit refused to die and she joined the many lost souls that are said to wander this area. Her heart is believed to wash up on the shore on occasion, but if you find it while beach-combing beware, for possessing it will bring you bad luck.

Above the beach, the long-dead citizens of Dunwich rise from their salty resting places to walk along the cliffs' frayed edges. Sometimes they have been seen here as incorporeal, shadowy figures that flit between worlds, nameless. Another anonymous figure is said to wander the cliff-tops here—although, why he stands apart from the shadowy figures is unclear. Perhaps he is from a different time. Like the forlorn Elizabethan sailor mentioned above, he too seems to be looking for something that he has lost. Also here, a 'nature spirit' is supposed to have been captured on camera, although, sadly, further details and the photograph itself eludes me.

But this place wasn't always sand, shingle and pebble and the ghostly sounds of invisible cattle moving across the beach and roads of the area presumably indicate where the green and fertile pastures were once found.

In addition, there is a "sinister reputation" attached to the crumbling remains of the old leper hospital's chapel, with shadowy, "malformed figures" having been witnessed flitting through the roofless ruins after dark. The leper hospital was originally constructed far inland of Dunwich to keep the terrible disease from spreading. Now, the ruins of it are barely two hundred yards from the coast.

Similar shadows have been spotted at Greyfriars Priory, along with mysterious lights and the sounds of monks chanting.

There is yet another interesting tragedy attached to Dunwich and it recounts a theme that is common in hauntings; that of a love denied. A young nobleman was forbidden to marry the servant girl he had fallen for. He scoured the nearby woods for a last glimpse of her, but to no avail: she had been taken away. Day after day he returned to watch for her, but never could he find even the most subtle sign of her presence. Eventually, he dropped dead of a broken heart. Even today, it is said that this poor unfortunate soul stalks through the woodland beyond Dunwich and the lowland heath that lies nearby, ever searching for his missing love amid the "dark, tangled forest [that is] wrapped in a veil of secrecy".

A phantom Victorian horseman atop a fine Arab steed also roams this heath, but only when the moon is full. He is thought to belong to the Barne family who once owned large tracts of land in these parts.

In this area too, there are dangers that are not of this world. Impish, mischievous beings called hobby lanterns abound. They look to lead unwary travellers astray on the heaths and marshes and have long been associated with the region. They seem rather similar to the more well-known 'will-o'-the-wisp' or 'pixie-light'. Science insists that they are most likely to be naturally-produced methane that combines with phosphorus and spontaneously combusts, but that rather takes the fun out things, doesn't it?

As if this area wasn't already drenched in folklore and the supernatural enough, it is also linked to one of Britain's most enduring and infamous mysteries: that of the demonic hound, 'Black Shuck'. Like Whitby's Barguest, and as seems to be the case for most of this island's many Hell hound legends, Black Shuck also has a variety of aliases to draw upon: Galley Trot, Phantom Hound, Old Shock—and many more besides.

Also up in the air is whether the fearsome demon dog with large, wickedly curved fangs and eyes that glow like twin fiery coals is actually evil or not. Some say he appears as a messenger of doom, while others insist that he is actually a benign, protective force. Peter Underwood wrote of Black Shuck in his 1998 book, *This Haunted Isle*, saying that people who are quick to deny the beast's existence should, "Tell that to the local people."

In more recent times, the Ship Inn, a lovely little pub at Dunwich, has experienced a ghost in its attic. A landlady saw the ghost in question sitting on the end of her bed one night. It got up and walked into the wall, vanishing exactly where a bricked-up door was later uncovered.

And it isn't just on dry land that spectres and weird things abound, for it is said that Dunwich's underwater ruins are home to more than the usual sea-life that you'd expect to find. For here, beneath the waves, spectres and phantoms haunt this now sub-aquatic suburb as they do the land above. Even experienced divers have reported feeling as though they were 'not alone' while exploring the seabed.

Of course, it is very likely that most of these stories are nothing more that tall tales woven by idle tongues. Some of them have no doubt been passed down through generations of local residents and augmented by successive storytellers, while others were perhaps invented by the area's many smugglers with the intention of keeping prying eyes away from the beaches and hideouts that they used in plying their illicit trades. But, whether you believe that the stories embracing Dunwich are true or not, England's miniature version of Atlantis and the rich history that clings to a coastline ever gnawed by the sea remains as enchanting as it is fascinating. It is quite easy then to see how this land inspired writers of ghost fiction such as M.R. James and even today continues to enthuse both paranormalists and folklorists alike.

5

The Horrors of Highgate Cemetery

*Tales of vampires, phantoms and strange magical practices
abound in this sleepy London cemetery.*

The steep walk up to Highgate Cemetery first offers the
visitor one of London's greenest havens: Waterlow Park.
This historic space was given to the public in 1889 by the
philanthropist and politician, Sir Sydney Waterlow, to be a
sort of "garden for the gardenless". Nowadays, with its
tree-lined paths, sparkling ponds and lush plant-life it
provides a verdant introduction to Highgate, for the
Cemetery's imposing gothic entrances stand just a short
hop across Swain's Lane.

And here then, rambling across twenty acres is the
world famous Cemetery itself. Opened in 1839 after the
demolition of Ashworth House, Highgate Cemetery
quickly became a trendy resting place amongst well-to-do
Victorians. As such, it proved to be a very popular place to
be interred. In time, about 170,000 burials were divided
between the east and west sections.

In death, as in life, wealthy families sought to outdo
each other with ever more ornate gravestones and showy
mausoleums. It wasn't just the masonry that flourished,

either. Like Waterlow Park, Highgate was envisioned as a tranquil green space, a 'garden cemetery', punctuated by ornamental trees and sculpted gardens; a place where Londoners could get away from the hard toil and cloying grime of industry and experience a sort of peace amid the resting dead. For those reasons it became a much admired and oft-visited part of the capital.

As you'd expect, there are many notable people laid to rest in this Victorian necropolis: Karl Marx, George Eliot and Michael Faraday, to name but three.

But, despite Highgate's illustrious history, by the middle of the twentieth century this once glorious cemetery had been all but abandoned. Neglect allowed the plants to grow without course; wild flowers poked through cracks in tombstones, bending their stems to catch the sunlight; once-manicured trees spread their limbs with abandon; roots squeezed into masonry and widened crumbling fissures. Some tombs were slowly embraced by flora, while others were overrun entirely and disappeared under greenery. The previously immaculate cemetery was swamped by vegetation of all kinds. Here, the weed became king.

Fauna joined flora too; with birds, rabbits and foxes moving in where humans had moved out—well, *living* humans, anyway.

Then, in 1975, a group called The Friends of Highgate Cemetery was formed by local residents with an aim to sort out the place. Thanks to much hard work on their part, some of the Cemetery's former glory has now been restored and it has become one of Britain's most beautiful and important heritage sites. It is also, reputedly, one of the most haunted locations in the country, for it is said that, even in daylight, ghosts walk here—and if the many stories about them are to be believed, they are many in number.

The Egyptian Avenue especially seems to be a draw for spirits with a multitude of apparitions being seen flitting across or along it. Amongst their numbers is the long-haired apparition of an elderly woman that wanders around the gravestones. She is sometimes described as mad, although quite what behaviour she evinces to make witnesses assume this is not usually described. Those that speak of her insanity put it down to the rumour that she murdered her children and now flits through the Cemetery searching for them. Could she be the one who delights in throwing small stones about and lightly touches visitors' arms? Perhaps that is the shrouded figure that people have reported, the one that stares into the distance and vanishes if anyone gets too close.

People have also reported feeling "cold touches" and hearing disembodied voices around this section. There's also the ghost of a small dog here. He hangs forlornly around Elizabeth Siddal's grave (more on her later). Others witnesses have described feeling an intense sensation of being watched—but might this be a natural sensation to experience when in a large, thought-provoking graveyard?

Apparitions and strange things aren't limited to the space within Highgate Cemetery's acres. Just outside, a spectral cyclist has been seen pedalling hard up Highgate Hill while some unfortunate locals have witnessed a tall man in a top hat who, on occasion, strolled nonchalantly across the road and then disappeared into a nearby wall. His nebulous meandering was, they said, always accompanied by a mournful tolling from the bells in an old disused chapel nearby.

An interesting encounter with this smartly dressed fellow took place only recently. *The Haringey Independent* reported in June 2012 that three members of North London Paranormal Investigations were out in the Cemetery around 10pm, when a "tall, dark figure" came into view. Micky Gocool, Louise Roche and Gemma Louise Pugh were walking in the area when Mr. Gocool, who has been helping Highgate residents with their paranormal concerns for many years, felt a delicate pinch on one of his arms. Surprised, he looked around and saw the strange figure standing close by. Its smart appearance matched previous witness reports and lead the group to think he might have been an undertaker in life. Mr. Gocool commented, saying that he could sense that the figure was not in any way threatening and, actually, despite looking rather pale and gaunt, he was "a normal, average Joe Public".

The ghost hung around for just a few seconds before disappearing.

Sometime around 1970, a man whose car had broken down near to the Cemetery saw "a hideous apparition with glowing red eyes, glaring at him through the rusting iron gates". Another, who was nipping through the Cemetery on a shortcut home, discovered "an imp-like creature" darting about amid the graves. Yet another chap who was walking along Swain's Lane, was thrown to the ground by "a fearsome creature that seemed to glide from the wall of the cemetery". With almost perfect timing, the unnamed man was "saved by the headlights of an approaching car that seemed to cause the 'thing' to dissolve into thin air". Sources disagree as to a conclusive identification of the gender of the person in this story.

The ghosts of Dante Gabriel Rossetti and Charles Dickens seem to be popular sightings here; this is in spite of the fact that they are both buried elsewhere. Dickens has close family buried in the Cemetery, so it could be that which draws his spirit to this place. Rossetti too has family here, but I think it is more likely to be Elizabeth Siddal's grave that claims some kind of otherworldly hold over Rossetti. Siddal was a model for many Pre-Raphaelite painters and much-loved by Rossetti. She was at first his muse and later became his wife, and her relatively early death at the age of 32 devastated him.

Beset by deep grief and heartache, Rossetti decided to leave one of his notebooks in Elizabeth's coffin, to be buried alongside her as a token of his everlasting love. The book contained many of his poems—some of which he possessed no copies of.

Years later, when Rossetti was under a cloud of depression, his agent, a somewhat reviled fellow by the name of Charles Augustus Howell, convinced him to have Siddal exhumed and the notebook retrieved for publishing. To avoid bad publicity, this gruesome task was carried out at night under the veil of darkness. Legend has it that the men who were present saw that Siddal was "remarkably well preserved and her delicate beauty intact", and "that the coffin was filled with her flowing coppery hair". Sadly, the exhumation was rather in vain, as the subsequent publication of the notebook's poems was not well received and Rossetti became haunted by the decision to dig up his lover for the rest of his life.

Even more infamous than Rossetti's sad tale are the stories that surround the Vampire of Highgate.

In the late 1960s, when Highgate was still overgrown, vandalised and unloved (a perfect setting for a number of Hammer Productions' horror films), a group of young people interested in the occult began to visit it after dark. Their presence did not go unnoticed and rumours whispered that a "sinister cult" had made the abandoned cemetery its home. Soon, a local newspaper called *The Hampstead and Highgate Express* began to receive letters from its readers telling of all manner of ghostly encounters connected with the cemetery. Highgate was edging back into the public's consciousness.

The group of young occultists had named themselves the *British Psychic and Occult Society*. On the 21st of December, 1969, one of the founder members of this group, David Farrant, claimed to have seen a dark figure while passing by Highgate Cemetery. He was certain that what he'd discovered was of supernatural origin. He related the story of his encounter to Yoav Harel in a 1998 interview:

> "In 1969, after reports of an unexplained
> entity at Highgate Cemetery, I went to visit it
> myself. It was late one evening—after

Christmas as a matter of fact—and I noticed a tall, dark shape just inside the gate and it seemed to be hovering above the ground—and it was real, at least it was so real I thought it was real.

"At first, I thought it was somebody dressed up inside the cemetery who was there trying to frighten people, but I soon changed my mind because when I looked closely it didn't have any discernible features, but there were two red points of light—orangey, red light—which were suspended in a black sort of shape which I took to be its face. The immediate area turned icy cold. I felt I was being drained of energy; under psychic attack.

"There are ways of protecting yourself against such things and I recited the cabbalistic invocation—only mentally, of course—and the thing—well, all of a sudden it wasn't there: it disappeared."

At this time, another local personality appeared on the Highgate scene. Seán Manchester believed that what David Farrant and others had witnessed in the Cemetery was in fact a bona fide vampire. Manchester claimed the vampire might be on the loose in Highgate, saying in an interview that, "there are others who amply attest to have been visited by it in their beds at night".

Interestingly, psychic investigator Farrant doubts that there was ever any such thing as a vampire at Highgate; at least not in the sense of a Stoker-esque blood-sucker. Instead, he suggests that the vampire was a hoax, perpetrated for publicity.

Despite a handful of common interests, Farrant and Manchester refused to see eye-to-eye, and even though they were both enthusiastic pursuers of this supernatural lurker—whatever it was—it seems that the two men quickly disliked each other. Publicity grew as their rivalry took root. Soon, the Highgate vampire seemed to become more about Farrant and Manchester than the vampire itself, and certainly to today's investigator their two names are ubiquitous when researching the area's many spooks and spectres.

So it seems likely then that this vampire was more of a media sensation than supernatural bloodsucker. But something enigmatic does keep cropping up in the area. Could it be that the tall figure Mickey Gocool saw is behind the so-called vampire appearances over the years?

It isn't just the Cemetery that boasts of ghosts. Highgate has had many weird and wonderful goings on over the centuries. Phantom horses that appear from banks of mist, haunted public houses and even a phantom chicken (yes, you read that right). Some people believe that a mystical ley runs through the area and it might be this that fuels the supernatural occurrences.

Ghostly goings-on aside, Highgate Cemetery remains a tranquil and beautiful place. One former tour guide said: "From the moment you step through the gates at Highgate, a great sense of peace washes over you. The sound of the wind in the trees and the sound of your own footsteps on the gravel courtyard all add to the atmosphere."

The Cemetery is privately owned and is operated by a non-profit making charity—the Friends of Highgate Cemetery. It receives no government funding at all, so every donation is important and goes towards the conservation of the Cemetery. The eastern section can be visited for a small fee but the western side can only be viewed during the guided tour. Sadly, the Friends does not reply to any correspondence of a supernatural nature whatsoever, which is a shame as a lack of an 'expert source' can sometimes help to give inaccurate or fictional stories a degree of longevity.

A caveat for any ghost hunters wishing to visit Highgate: the Cemetery is not only a grade one listed park but also a genuinely functioning place of rest with burials occurring most weeks. There is currently no 'ghost walk'.

6
The Skirrid Mountain Inn

Do the spirits of hanged men skulk within these ancient walls?

Lurking in the old rooms and dim corners of the Skirrid Inn there are creatures of darkness. Ghostly footsteps make centuries-old floorboards creak in the night. Long-dead soldiers rally in the courtyard, steeling themselves for battles already fought. Doors open and close by themselves, or rattle on their hinges without aid from a living hand. Shouts of "Don't kill me!" echo along the corridors...

This aged inn sits in the Welsh county of Monmouthshire, in the small village of Llanvihangel Crucorney (in Welsh, Llanfihangel Crucornau), not far from the border with England. Further south stands Ysgyryd Fawr, the most easterly peak of the range of hills named the Black Mountains.

Ysgyryd Fawr, owned by the National Trust, is also known by another name—the Holy Mountain. A local legend tells of a great storm that raged and smashed the peak in two at the exact time of Jesus Christ's crucifixion, thus leading to the mount's distinctive outline. Because of this holy connection, soil from the Mountain was long considered to have sacred properties and many people travelled to the area to take some away for their fields and stables and to scatter in the foundations of new buildings in the hope of bringing good fortune and health.

Another interesting geographical feature, Offa's Dyke, runs close by, predating the Inn by hundreds of years. This earthwork, many miles long, is attributed in the main to the powerful Mercian King Offa. It was a considerable defensive construction in its day, snaking across the Welsh and English border, and even today still retains its original dimensions in some places.

Named for its view of Ysgyryd Fawr (when Anglicised, *Ysgyryd* becomes *Skirrid*), the Skirrid Inn stands solidly upon stone walls hewn from Old Red Sandstone—rocks that were most probably quarried from around the Ysgyryd Fawr's footprint as the Black Mountains contain such ancient, Devonian Period stuff.

Inside the building, old wood panelling adorns some of the walls, while oak beams—said to have been salvaged from a Tudor warship and inclusive of their original slots and peg holes—support the ceiling. There's even an old ship's bell for calling last orders at the bar of this grade two listed public house.

In the forecourt, aged stone mounting steps still hug one of the Inn's walls. They have helped many a traveller into their saddles—perhaps even kings, some say.

One person who might have used them is Owain Glyndŵr. He was an Anglo-Welsh nobleman who fought a long war against the English control of Wales. Ultimately, he was unsuccessful, but it is said that his spirit lingers on here and the apparitions of his followers have been reported riding out from the courtyard with the intention of attacking their enemies. The clattering of an invisible horse's hooves have also been heard cantering past the Inn.

The reported paranormal phenomena inside the Skirrid Inn make up a substantial list.

Fanny Price

Of all of the Inn's supernatural residents, the most likely to be encountered is said to be Fanny Price. Together with her husband Henry she ran the pub in the mid-to-late 1800s. Said to have been a strong woman, she died of consumption (what we might call pulmonary tuberculosis today) in the September of 1875 and is buried with Henry and five others of her family in the nearby churchyard. By all accounts a fairly happy soul, her spirit is supposed to be quite active, mostly in Room 3, and she is often accompanied by the aroma of lavender. Henry is thought to be behind the strange banging noises that are sometimes heard coming from the chimney breasts.

Despite generally being amiable, Fanny is supposed to have a mischievous side.

Some years ago, a girl was taking a bath in one of the guest bedrooms (Room 1) when she was forced under the water and held there by invisible hands. The story goes that the girl was so terrified that when she managed to free herself she jumped out of the bath and ran downstairs clad only in a towel and coat. Still soaked, she told the landlord, Geoff Fiddler, that somebody—a female—had tried to murder her in the bath.

In the same room two taps have turned on simultaneously of their own accord.

Could all this have been Fanny's doing? If not her actions, then maybe it is the work of the 'white lady' whose rustling dress and accompanying chill have been sensed by staff and guests alike.

Or perhaps it is more likely to be the evil female presence that has been sensed upon the stairs; a location that also offers visitors the chance to experience feelings of unexplained terror, strange shadows, intense nausea and dizziness.

As you might expect, sleeping overnight in the Inn can be an interesting experience for some guests. One such patron reported the toilet roll spinning by itself all night. Another woke to find a dark figure standing at the bottom of his bed. On one occasion, an Australian man was roused in the early morning, freezing cold despite the heating being on. He could hear snoring noises emanating from where his girlfriend was sleeping—only it wasn't her doing the snoring and there was nobody else in the room.

Downstairs, the bar isn't immune from such paranormal perils, either. Here, glasses have a rather short life-span as they seem to "fly off the bar unaided by human hands", according to Siani Thomas of the blog Strange Days. Some sources write that as many as fifteen glasses are lost in this way on a weekly basis. Equally bizarrely, over a period of ten minutes, a £10 note with three £1 coins resting on it slid across the bar while shocked onlookers watched from their seats. The note continued off the bar's edge, floated briefly in the air and then dropped to the floor.

Also in the bar an interesting old practice is to be found; one that is aimed at appeasing the Devil himself. In the early evening a cup of ale is set aside, usually placed by the fireplace, just in case Old Nick pops in for a drink. Similarly, an older custom took place outside when the veil of night had fallen across the land and the final drinkers were staggering back to their homes. Just before locking up for the evening, the landlord would set a cup outside on the Inn's doorstep, but this one wasn't for the Devil, instead it was meant for the shape-shifting pwca (or pwwka)—a mysterious fairy or goblin-like creature of ambiguous intent. How often it was sneakily supped by late-night travellers is not known.

Amongst the many spirits, knocking sounds, strange lights, slamming and rattling doors, cold spots, object aportation (especially jewellery and the like), and weird footsteps there wanders a holy man. Father Henry Vaughn—a friendly spirit—has somehow become tethered to the property. I wonder if he used to be linked to the nearby Llanvihangel Crucorney Church. Sadly, details of Father Vaughn are scant.

The Noose, Rebels and Hanging Judge Jeffreys

With all this phenomena going on, you might imagine a grisly story of some kind is lurking in the background. Well, you'd be right, for the Inn's most gruesome claim to fame is its hangings—one hundred and eighty of them, to be precise.

Supposedly, between the twelfth and seventeenth centuries, the Inn's upstairs rooms were used as a court. Boundary disputes, the resolution of local arguments and ownership matters were all dealt with. As were men who broke the law. For their transgressions, some of those men paid the ultimate price.

One such chap was called John Crowther. Sometime around 1100 (when some writers say that the Inn was called the 'Millbrook'), he and his brother James were put up before the court; John for stealing sheep and James for an act of violent robbery. James received a sentence of nine months imprisonment and John was taken away to be hanged—some say his was the first execution at the Inn.

Over the centuries almost two hundred more hangings were carried out, with a wooden beam over the stairwell acting as a gibbet. And there was no 'long drop and short stop' to be found here, either, as the rope's length wasn't long enough to break the neck cleanly. A drawn-out strangulation was the grim order of the day. Halfway up the Inn's square spiral staircase is the small room that acted as the cell. It is now used as a simple store room.

Some of those hanged are said to have been rebels who had taken up arms against King James II during the Monmouth Rebellion of 1685. With the notorious 'Hanging' Judge Jeffreys presiding over the courtroom proceedings, many of the rebels were hanged from the Inn's notorious stairwell beam. Judge Jeffreys' apparition is rumoured to stalk the building's upper floors. The last person to be executed here was hanged "on the instructions of Oliver Cromwell"; like John Crowther, his crime was sheep rustling.

In the early 1960s, one man claimed to have heard the

last words of one of those hanged in the stairwell. G. Jones worked for the architect's department at Rhymney Breweries when it owned the Skirrid. He writes: "Together with Alwyn Morgan, I was in the premises and on the staircase. We both heard screams and shouts of, 'Don't kill me!' We had not been drinking. We were shaken. Perhaps it was Crowther that shouted, 'Don't kill me!'"

With stories like this floating about, it's little wonder that visitors have described other strange feelings, like those of being strangled, and even that scarlet rope burns have appeared around their throats, as if from out of nowhere.

The beam—or more likely a later replacement—stands today and it bears chaffing and scorch marks from the hangman's rope.

The British Isles seems to be something of a breeding ground for haunted pubs. Those claiming to possess spirits of the undead kind number in their hundreds, if not thousands. Perhaps this is because pubs and similar hostelries played such important roles in the communities of centuries gone by, becoming genuine epicentres of everyday life, and as such were hosts to a wide variety of interesting and important events—from celebrations to murders. Have the strong emotions caused by such events become recorded within the fabric of such buildings (the 'stone tape theory')? Or are 'ghosts' more likely to be reported in public houses because of the telling of tall tales and exaggerated adventures that takes place amongst ale-supping friends? Maybe, in reality, it is because everyone is always drunk...

If the stone tape theory (that events and emotions can become recorded somehow by nearby materials and replayed at a later date under certain conditions) has any truth to it, the Skirrid Inn surely fits the bill when it comes to the pervasion of powerful emotions. The anguish and terror that must have been felt by those 180 criminals, as they each waited in the Inn's cramped cell overnight, listening to the revelry going on below them—some perhaps innocent of their crimes—must have been nightmarish. Torment indeed. Is it unsurprising then, that some portion of those doomed personalities still linger on here in one form or another?

But, what if there were no hangings at the Skirrid Inn?

Without doubt, all might not be as it at first seems in this Welsh public house, for when you scratch the surface of the Skirrid Inn's notorious history, not everything sits quite as nicely as it should. Initially, most sources regarding the Inn's bloody past corroborate each other, but it soon becomes apparent that rather than backing each other up with independent research, they simply regurgitate the same stories from the same core sources and provide little in the way of historical evidence. There is a distinct paucity of real excavation.

The pub is said to date back to about the year 1110, with most print and online sources mentioning that this date has been verified by 'Welsh chronicles', 'legal records' or 'historical records'. But, frustratingly, not one of these sources actually seems to give a proper name for these records, leaving those who want to find out more in the dark.

Add in the dubious nature of some of the stories on offer, such as John Crowther's brother James being sentenced to nine months imprisonment at a time when prison did not really exist as a punishment (prisons generally being extant only for the purpose of holding those awaiting trial), and the waters muddy considerably. Additionally, it is of course *possible* that Judge Jeffreys might have visited the Inn—he did travel about the country a fair bit—and perhaps he even held court here, but it is very strange to claim that he hanged Monmouth rebels from the Inn's beam. Not least because the uprising's main battle (the Battle of Sedgemore) and the subsequent trials took place largely in the south of England—the West Country in particular. Could it be that someone in the Inn's past simply confused the county of Monmouthshire with the Duke of Monmouth and assumed that the rebellion was connected with this part of Wales?

Furthermore, the Skirrid Inn's claim that it dates back to around the year 1110 is also not quite as clear cut as most sources seem to insist. The Glamorgan-Gwent Archaeological Trust's historic environment records offer up a different side to the story with their description, dating the present building as a more modern construction:

> "A mid-late 17th century building which appears to have been purpose-built as an inn. Major alterations took place to the fabric in 19th century, and minor alterations in the 20th century. The main surviving features from 17th century are the main timbers of the roof, the ceilings of the principal downstairs rooms and the fine oak staircase which extends from the ground floor to the attics, and has its own tower. The main door and door-frame also date back to this period, but with some parts of them replaced.
>
> "Although the exterior has a 17th century appearance, this is largely the result of the 19th century rebuilding, which replaced all the windows in a 17th century style. This building is popularly supposed to be of medieval origin, but there is no evidence for anything earlier than 17th century."

One claim, that the old mounting stone has been used by many of England's past kings is particularly outlandish. No evidence seems to exist of monarchs ever having reason for visiting the pub. Also in the cobbled courtyard, if Glamorgan-Gwent's archaeological records are to be believed, unless older pre-existing parts of the Skirrid Inn were retained during the mid-to-late 1600s rebuild, the mounting block and courtyard couldn't have been used by

Owain Glyndŵr at all as he disappeared, thought dead, around 1412.

Of course, having said that, retention of older features and the reuse of original building materials is not at all unlikely and some studies and individuals have speculated that the Inn might sit on a larger, older site. This is especially plausible when you consider that it is situated on an old route that was used by pilgrims while journeying to Llanthony Abbey. The Abbey dates back to the year 1108 and even before that a chapel dedicated to St. David stood on the site, so pilgrims might have been making their way through Llanvihangel Crucorney for well over a thousand years, and if not in use by pilgrims then certainly the drovers and other travellers that have long walked the road have needed a place to rest their weary bones.

So there is a confident case for the Inn's claim of being one of the oldest around, even if the evidence is not exactly apparent.

But what of the ghosts?

One descendant of Henry and Fanny Price claims that some of the ghost stories were actually made up by his father in the early 1950s. At that time, the Skirrid Inn was being run by a relative and so his father would travel there to drink. He writes:

> "My father had at the time returned from national service in Ethiopia and was [in the Skirrid Inn] with his mates engaging in a drinking binge. As the topic of the Devil's cup came up my father invented the story of the hangings for a laugh to scare his army mates who were staying there. The legend sort of slowly took off from there."

And those grooves and burn marks in the beam over the staircase? Well according to the same source they were not made by the kicks and struggles of dying men, instead they came about when pigs were being slaughtered inside the building—"strung up by their hind legs and their throats were cut".

So, was the Skirrid's bloody history of executions merely concocted (or exaggerated) by some of the establishment's previous owners in order to get more customers through the door?

While it almost certainly was used as a place to hold the local manorial courts that dealt with the administration of the surrounding holdings, boundary disputes and so on, sadly, as court leet records for the Barony of Abergavenny only exist from 1767 onwards, and, as the last hanging supposedly took place during Oliver Cromwell's time (he was in office from the 16th of December, 1653, to the 3rd of September, 1658), it is quite possible that we might never know if there really were 180 hangings at the Inn.

At least one record exists of a trial being held at Llanvihangel Crucorney, though. On the 10th of June, 1804, one James Bennison stood accused of stealing a horse which he later sold at Hay Fair. Where this trial took place is not known, but the Inn makes for a likely setting.

Certainly, the personal experiences of many people support the idea that the building is haunted, and without doubt, there have been many strange events reported over the years with some corroborating others via hidden knowledge. A past landlady, Heather Grant, described her experiences of the ghosts: "There have been lots of spooky goings-on since I've been here. I live on my own, and when I first moved in, I have to confess that I was pretty unnerved by things happening. Despite everything that happens here, you get used to it, and I don't mind them anymore."

The Skirrid Inn, with its charming character and fascinating past, continues to attract tourists and ghost hunters each year. Visitors are understandably spellbound by the macabre stories, rural location and sheer age of the place. Whether aspects of the Inn's past are true or false, it remains that the pub is a cosy, much-loved and memorable establishment. A genuine step back in time set against a stunning backdrop.

7
The South Bridge Vaults

What terrors lurk in the gloom beneath Scotland's ancient capital city?

Edinburgh is something of a fright-fest. With Greyfriars Kirkyard, the Black Mausoleum, Mary King's Close and a whole host of other purportedly haunted locations it seems as though Scotland's capital city is utterly riddled with the mysterious and the macabre. And it is to one of *Auld Reekie's* creepiest gems that we turn our attention to now, because, deep beneath one of the city's oldest streets is a place darker than Lord Voldemort's trousers—and so infamous that it beckons ghost hunters from across the planet to explore its murky depths. For these are the abandoned vaults that lie underneath the South Bridge: a centuries-old underground network of tunnels and chambers that remains inextricable from the grim and grisly side of the city's long history.

The Vault's uneven, musty passageways run with rivulets of damp and provide a cold canvas for mildew, lichen and other hardy plants to adhere to. Down here, hardly any sunlight penetrates. Where the moisture has been allowed to collect over centuries, small stalactites have formed, clinging to the ceilings and giving the corridors a cavern-like ambience. It has been said that surely, if ghosts do exist, they would prowl the quiet shadows of the South Bridge Vaults.

In the latter years of the 1700s, Edinburgh began to blossom. The city's population swelled greatly and expansion became a necessity, but Edinburgh's hilly situation gave its civic planners a slew of problems. Amongst the solutions was a proposal for the building of two great bridges: the North Bridge and the South Bridge. First put forward in the 1752 pamphlet *Proposals for Carrying on Certain Public Works in the City of Edinburgh*, the latter would span the Cowgate gorge and link up with Nicolson Street. The architect Robert Kay would design it with the initial involvement of the then very fashionable (and native Edinburghian) Robert Adams. It would cost an estimated £8,300 and become one of the main thoroughfares for those entering Edinburgh from southern Scotland and England.

The Bridge was designed to be efficient with space and below its 'deck level' a hive of vaults were opened up in the arches to be used as storage for the rows of shops and businesses that occupied the flanks of its main street at the surface. Then, its nineteen arches were enclosed by high tenements and other buildings on each side, making the South Bridge look like any other street and hiding the true scope of its span. Even today, many visitors are unaware that they are actually walking across a bridge over a gorge.

The year 1790 would see the South Bridge complete, but it would also see a grim beginning and an ill-omen for the structure. As part of the grand opening, it was decided that one of the area's most well-liked residents—a judge's wife—should be the first to ride across it. The problem was that the judge's wife was also one of the area's most elderly citizens and, alas, she expired shortly before she was supposed to carry out her civic duty; a most untimely demise to say the least! The organisers went ahead regardless and her body was placed in a hearse to be carried across in the place of honour. Some saw this as a dark portent of things to come and superstitious ripples spread around the city. The South Bridge, it seemed, was jinxed from the very outset.

As planned, wealthy merchants of all kinds moved into this newly fashionable area regardless of any hearsay. Jewellers and book-binders rubbed shoulders with bankers and lawyers, while pedestrians wandered down the street and spent their money. But below the street trouble was brewing.

It seemed as though, despite Edinburgh's world-wide reputation for excellence in civil engineering, the vaults that had been built into the bridge's arches had not been properly water-proofed and now dampness and flooding began to cause unavoidable problems. Soon, the respectable milliners, cobblers, grocers and other businesses that had used the vaults left, with some of the chambers being abandoned to the rising water levels.

The owners sought new tenants for the vaults, but only poor families and those plying less reputable commercial enterprises were prepared to live in a sunless place that offered no running water and little legroom. For the next three decades, so things continued, until the conditions below ground worsened so much that even the brothels and gambling dens sought better quality accommodation.

With rent now reduced to the cheapest of rates, the very poorest of the city moved in; and with them came the lowest criminal classes. The dark, dangerous vaults made excellent places in which to store contraband or stolen goods. Even those infamous resurrectionists William Burke and William Hare were said to use the dark warren beneath the South Bridge to aid their ghastly deeds. The two Williams were the most active body snatchers of their day, hunting out freshly buried corpses to sell to Edinburgh's doctors for dissection. This practice was illegal enough, but in addition the duo was not against hastening the living to a premature demise if it made them money—preying mainly on women and the vulnerable. In the end, seventeen murders were committed by the two Irishmen in a spate that became known as the West Port Murders.

> *Up the close and down the stair,*
> *In the house with Burke and Hare.*
> *Burke's the butcher, Hare's the thief*
> *Knox, the man who buys the beef.*

As the deteriorating state of the vaults hastened, so it also became a breeding ground for disease. It must have been a truly miserable place for those that dwelt there—musty, damp and rife with crime, death and sickness. Like many similar slums it became what G.H. Martin called "a social trap from which there was no escape but death".

Some sources say that by around 1820, even the criminals had finally had enough and left the vaults. An accurate date for the sealing of the vaults is elusive, but sealed they were—by tons of earth and rubble. They were abandoned utterly and soon forgotten by the city around them.

Then, in the late 1980s, a former Scottish rugby player called Norrie Rowan discovered a tunnel that happened to link up to the South Bridge's vaults. With his son, Norman, he dug the tunnel out, shifting large amounts of rock and soil and discovering old toys, shells, bottles and other signs of previous habitation. By accident, the South Bridge Vaults had been rediscovered. Exploration revealed that some of the tunnels and chambers still existed in their original, grimy form.

In 1994 they were reopened to the public.

Some have said that the South Bridge Vaults' wretched history has led to it becoming nothing less than infested with all manner of frightening paranormal activity. Perhaps this is why the ghost tours that venture down into the South Bridge's gloom have proved so popular amongst visitors to Edinburgh. With all the strangers invading the darkness, it's no wonder that a great deal of phenomena has been reported over the years. Some of those reports are rather chilling.

One fascinating story involved two Canadian backpackers who noticed the cover had come off a shaft opening on nearby Niddry Street. Having heard the tales about Edinburgh's underground tunnels, they rightly guessed the shaft would lead down to the South Bridge's notorious vaults. Squeezing in, they found themselves in an old jeweller's storeroom. The room was vacant and dark, with the only illumination coming from the opening behind them. The two bravely set off on what they must have hoped would be an adventure: "Through the open door their flashlights revealed crumbling vaults stretching in every direction."

On and on they went, exploring the chambers and dank corridors. Until, almost simultaneously, both of their torches stopped working. Suddenly, the backpackers were plunged into an impenetrable darkness.

When the torches refused to respond, the pair at first kept their calm and decided to try to retrace their footsteps. They stumbled along, feeling their way back the way they had come, hoping to catch sight of the reassuring light coming from the shaft in the jeweller's storeroom. But no matter how hard they searched they couldn't find it. Panic set in.

They tripped and fell and screamed for help, but nobody above ground could hear them. For what seemed like hours they staggered through the blackness.

Eventually—purely by luck—they found their way back to the jeweller's storeroom, but only to discover that somebody had replaced the cover over the shaft. Their frantic calls were finally heard by a nearby pedestrian who was able to take off the cover and help the Canadians to sunlight and safety.

Now once more in the daylight, the two Canadians were in for a second shock: their faces were covered in claw-like scratches.

As for what could have made those scratches, well

quite a few restless spirits are said to inhabit the gloom of the vaults, and they manifest in many different ways. In fact, if you believe everything you read, the list of weird goings-on down there is almost endless. There have been whispered, disembodied words heard; shadows seen flitting around the small chambers; sensations of being touched; sudden drops in temperature felt; objects thrown about or seen moving of their own accord; and, of course, full-blown figures have been spotted.

One of these figures is a fellow called Mr. Boots. So-named because of his penchant for stomping loudly down the corridors as if wearing heavy boots, this ghost has the most fearsome reputation of all of the Vaults' supernatural denizens. The invasion of his home by tourists is said to anger him, as do lights, and he stalks about the chambers and passageways brandishing a knife or broken bottle. He is thought to have been a slum landlord in life—and a killer too, having murdered at least one young prostitute. His appearance is said to be a powerful one: tall of stature with a long dark coat, a "leering grin" and eyeless orbits. Shouts of "Get out!" have been heard and the formidable Mr. Boots is said to be the source.

Perhaps Mr. Boots is also behind the many cold spots that are "painful to the flesh" and seem to only affect women. These cold spots are especially strange as the vaults are not quite as chilly as one would first suspect, usually being relatively warm all year round—even during the Scottish winter.

Then there's the boy, Jack, who is a much more welcoming presence. He sometimes waves at people and throws small stones. He also holds their hands while they are on the tours. At least one psychic has said that Jack, in life, disappeared down here around 1810. Sadly, of him, no more details are known. In what has been called the 'leather room', people have reported seeing a phantom cobbler still at work. Like Jack, he is a largely amiable spirit, quite dissimilar to the inhabitant of one of the other corners of this room. She is a young woman of about twenty, who wears a black veil and likes to push around female visitors, especially if they are pregnant. Perhaps she mourns the loss of a child of her own.

Another story of interest comes to us from Jan-Andrew Henderson's indispensible book about subterranean Edinburgh, *The Town Below the Ground*. Back in 1996, a coven of witches intended to use a chamber in the vaults as a temple. They chose one of the warmest, driest rooms; one that their leader—a man named George Cameron— claimed had a noticeable degree of psychic energy about it. A mirror was needed for some of their rituals and a large one was taken from an old wardrobe door and placed in a corner. It was this addition that would evaporate whatever welcoming feeling the room might have had:

> "At first everything seemed normal—at least as normal as a pagan temple can be. The coven had the use of the vault for rituals late at night. (They were white witches so no devil worship or human sacrifice was going on.) Then things began to go wrong.
>
> "The coven leader himself was the first to be alarmed. He had always insisted he could feel long-dead spirits wandering through the vaults—but they had always been friendly. Now he sensed a new and very different presence. Something evil, he insisted, had invaded the vaults. To challenge this entity he prepared to spend the night alone in his temple."

In the middle of the night, the brave coven leader sensed that something was not quite as it should be. He saw shifting shadows near the mirror, as if an 'entity' was crawling about. He uttered protective chants into the darkness and then settled down, apparently making it through the rest of the night without interruption.

Whatever was lurking within the chamber seemed to be

growing in power. Over the following weeks and days, visitors told of sudden, "terrifying" temperature drops.

One quote survives from a visitor who claimed to enjoy psychic abilities: "That isn't a mirror [...] it's a door. It's a door and it's letting in evil." Whether it was a doorway or not, the mirror certainly became the focus of fear. Multiple reports of a mysterious white figure that appeared to step out of and then back into the mirror were talked about. A general feeling of uneasiness pervaded and the once-dry walls ran with moisture that collected in a fetid pool near the mirror. Soon, the witches had had enough and they relocated their temple elsewhere. Jan-Andrew Henderson reports that the original temple vault went back to its original state almost as soon as the mirror and other accoutrements were removed, but the second temple was destined to go the same way as the first one:

> "As soon as it was moved, the old vault began to dry up. Within weeks all the water was gone.
>
> "The new pagan temple fared no better than the old one. On a number of occasions the mirror was found face down but unbroken on the stone floor—even though the new vault was locked. In the vault next door, a tour party experienced a sudden temperature drop. Two children, aged three and four, began to cry and pointed at a seemingly empty corner of the vault. They insisted that the 'man from the mirror' was frightening them."

The story ends with the mirror being discovered cracked one morning and then finally being discarded.

There are even said to be spirit animals down here under the streets of Edinburgh. A dog has been heard, its claws striking the stone floors as it scampers about. Additionally, and quite bizarrely, there has also been reported the impression of "something like a hawk about to swoop down from the ceiling" in one chamber.

Even the Cowgate Gorge itself has at least one spook; a shadowy man who was executed by hanging and now haunts the place of his death, still with discernible rope burns from the noose that choked away his life. He appears only at night.

So, has there been any actual, reliable evidence captured for all of this supposed phenomena? When the U.S. TV show *Ghost Adventures* visited they recorded dragging sounds that went on for nearly six minutes, unexplained noises, a strange female voice, weird knocking, noises that sounded as though they came from a dog, a child's voice and a teddy bear that appeared to rotate slightly of its own accord.

Furthermore, during the filming of a 2010 TV show called *Joe Swash Believes in Ghosts*, the production crew captured more mysterious voices on their recording equipment. Presenter Swash was left alone in the vaults overnight, with only a few cameras and microphones for company. While he didn't hear any voices himself, they were positively picked up by the equipment around him. Amongst them could be heard the words of a Catholic priest reading the Last Rites and the raised voices of children. After in-depth analysis of the audio files, no scientific explanation could be offered.

So, what could explain the phenomena down in the vaults? One explanation centres upon the South Bridge being heavily used by motor vehicles, and something called infrasound.

Infrasound is sound that is lower in frequency than that which humans can normally hear, but it can still sometimes be *felt*. The lecturer and engineer Vic Tandy researched infrasound and found that at some frequencies it was able to affect eyesight, emotions and even move inanimate objects.

In his 1998 paper, published in the Journal of the Society for Psychical Research, Tandy described his experience of working in what might have been considered to be a haunted medical research laboratory. Tandy knew that people had experienced strange things in the lab before, but it wasn't until he was working alone one night that he really sat up and took notice. As he wrote at his desk he began to feel more and more uncomfortable—as though there was some kind of presence in the room with him. Eventually, it started to feel like he was being watched. Then, out of the corner of his eye, a grey shape emerged. It seemed to take the form of a person.

Tandy was terrified, but he managed to summon up the courage to turn to look straight at the apparition. As he did so, it disappeared.

The next day he was in the lab repairing a fencing foil for a competition. He clamped the foil securely in a vice and went to look for something. When he came back he was surprised to see the foil's thin blade "frantically vibrating up and down": another bizarre occurrence. But this kind of thing was more in line with Tandy's expertise and so he began to look for what was making the blade move.

Much experimentation led to the discovery that a low frequency standing wave of 18.98 Hz was present in the lab. A search for what was emitting the standing wave uncovered that an extractor fan had recently been installed in a small cleaning room at the end of the lab. It was this machine that was creating the standing wave. When it was switched off, "it was as if a huge weight was lifted."

The frequency of the standing wave turned out to be the precise one needed to make the human eyeball vibrate minutely, with the area of greatest effect being close to Vic Tandy's desk. So the grey apparition was not a watching spirit, but in fact merely an optical illusion and the vibrating foil was another physical reaction to the present infrasound. Could it be that the vibrations from the heavy traffic on the road above the South Bridge are travelling into the vaults and affecting people who visit in a similar way to what was happening in Vic Tandy's lab?

Infrasound aside, might it simply be the power of suggestion that is conjuring up spectres? After all, the South Bridge Vaults are a perfect breeding ground for fear: a series of small enclosed spaces with a particularly miserable and gruesome history to go with them, not to mention that they are downright dark and dank, and have a plethora of well-known ghost stories attached.

In 2001, Professor Richard Wiseman and a number of volunteers took part in an experiment in some of the vaults. Participants were asked to spend about ten minutes alone in a vault and note down any strange things that might happen. The participants reported a total of 172 unusual experiences ranging from temperature drops, sensations of being watched, burning feelings, unusual sounds and aromas and also sightings of apparitions.

The experiment took into account both the participants' existing knowledge of the Vaults' reputation as a haunted location (or lack thereof) and environmental factors such as the temperature, lighting levels and the dimensions of each vault used.

The results showed that participants were more likely to report strange events if they believed in ghosts, and that more strange events were reported in the vaults that were thought to be particularly haunted and that the environmental factors played a not insignificant part in affecting participants.

So, in essence, people can 'help' to create hauntings through the way they perceive their surroundings.

Frankly, 'suggestion' simply has to affect visitors to the South Bridge Vaults, after all, this is an extremely spooky location and it is no great leap of the imagination to visualize the horrific experiences of those unfortunate people that once lived and died there. Especially so when tour guides talk in theatrical voices of witchcraft, body snatchers and ghosts. Add in the low lighting, the subterranean situation and a smattering of claustrophobia and you have a heady cocktail for nausea, dizziness, the assumption that sounds and smells are of an unnatural origin and many other things that people tend to report at so-called haunted sites.

Genuinely haunted or not, the South Bridge Vaults offer us a fascinating insight into just how grim life could be in 18th century Edinburgh: an authentic slice of gruesome history. One thing is for certain, no matter what the cause might be, eldritch happenings are going on down in those vaults.

8
The Spectre of the Silent Pool

Is the famous serenity of this pool tainted by the legacy of a medieval murder?

Within the heart of the southern county of Surrey, nestling in between the two picturesque villages of Shere and Albury, there is a place of mystery and fable. Set back a short distance from the winding Shere Road and somewhat hidden within a thicket of trees, the Silent Pool has long provided succour for those seeking tranquillity and quiet contemplation. But, while the serene and notably clear waters of the Pool offer solace to some, to others the place is tainted by the indelible legacy of a medieval murder.

A stone-strewn car park surrounds the understated entrance to a trail that leads first to Sherbourne Pond (the lower of the two pools) and then on to the Silent Pool itself. Once on the path, the sounds of traffic on the nearby road quickly become muted and suddenly there falls a natural peacefulness over the visitor. Overhead, tall trees arch above the sun-dappled, well-trodden pathway.

It isn't far to Sherbourne Pond where a viewing platform has been built overlooking the water and the babbling, trickling sound of the higher Pool draining into the pond through two streams and a culvert becomes noticeable. Here and there, lily pads compete with the clusters of algae for the warming sun's rays.

From the Pond, the path continues up a gentle incline and through a tunnel of Beech and Yew trees, and soon the corridor of branches and bushes gives way to reveal the clear waters of the Silent Pool. It is far more accessible than the Pond with a footpath snaking around its edge, and it's longer too; stretching away until its end is hidden by overhanging foliage. The air seems crisper here somehow and in late summer the warm sun reaches deep into the water and illuminates the emerald green plant life.

Despite the crunch of gravel and stones underfoot, the Silent Pool does its best to live up to its name, perhaps this is why the area has long been considered a site of mystery. Legends claim that no birds will sing in the trees while others suggest the Pool is actually dangerously bottomless in places.

And there is another, more infamous legend that has its roots here in this idyllic spot.

Many centuries ago, Emma, a young maiden from a nearby village, would visit the pool to bathe. During one of these dips she noticed that a strange man was watching her from atop his horse. Seeing that she had spotted him, he ushered his steed a few steps forward and revealed himself to be none other than that dastardly figure from English history—King John. Being a dignified sort, the young girl retreated away from his presence. But alas, her evasion brought her closer to the Pool's treacherous depths. The King saw this and advanced towards her, urging his mount into the waters with lecherous intent. As he neared her she stumbled to a part of the Pool that becomes deep abruptly and, unable to swim, she let out a panicked cry before slipping beneath the crystal clear waters.

The callous King made no move to save her and simply left the scene, failing to notice that an incriminating feather from his hat had become caught in one of the low-hanging branches that ringed the Pool. An addition to the tale suggests that the girl's brother heard her scream and raced to the scene. He plunged head first into the pool in an attempt to save her but he too drowned.

The story doesn't stop there.

The Archbishop of Canterbury, Stephen Langton, heard this tale of woe and resolved to do something about it. He himself had had a similar confrontation with King John many years before Emma's sad demise.

At the age of eighteen, Langton lived in nearby Albury. He had fallen in love with a beautiful girl called Alice. On a summer's walk through the woods that embrace the Silent Pool (no doubt much larger then than now), the two young lovers were suddenly set upon by "a band of thugs led by none other than Prince John". Langton was beaten until he was unconscious while Alice was dragged away by the ruffians. Fortunately, both Alice and Langton survived the attack, but assumed each other dead and both dedicated themselves to life within the church.

Langton's hatred for John caused him to lead a group of barons in revolt against the King. His "energetic leadership and the barons' military strength" forced King John to accept the signing of the Magna Carta at Runnymede in 1215.

On the surface, it's already an unlikely story and with a little research it soon becomes clear that the old tale is not authentic (or even that old). It was, in fact, penned by a writer named Martin Farquhar Tupper. Tupper has been called "one of the worst poets ever". He wrote *Stephen Langton - a Romance of the Silent Pool* in 1857 in order to "add a new interest to Albury and surrounding areas". Confusingly for modern-day researchers, Tupper decided to include real-life figures in his story: the eponymous Stephen Langton really was an Archbishop of Canterbury and really was at the head of the Barons' Revolt against King John. At one point it seems that Tupper also told a downright fib when he insisted that his work "may be depended upon for historical accuracy in every detail". As other sources suggest; it is now "impossible to tell what form the legend took before his time, if indeed it existed at all."

At one time Tupper was something of a household name, but now his works are largely forgotten by the public. His account of the drowning at the Silent Pool, though, has become inextricable from the area's history and even now local tales insist that Emma's ghost still returns to haunt the spot. People claim to have seen her spectral figure floating above the water's surface, or noiselessly disrobing before walking into the pool without a ripple. Horse's hooves, screams and desperate pleas for help have also been heard and even the terrible vision of a black-eyed rider emerging fiercely from a bank of mist has been reported.

While the veracity of Tupper's tale is very much clouded, a real-life mystery touched the Silent Pool in early December, 1926. The car of the world-famous novelist Agatha Christie was found "abandoned, covered in frost and with its headlights on" at nearby Newland's Corner. The authoress was nowhere to be seen.

Christie's husband, Archie, had recently requested an end to their marriage, the reason being that he had fallen in love with a young woman by the name of Nancy Neele. Things came to a head when Archie left his wife and went off to spend the weekend with Neele in nearby Godalming. This domestic rift was thought to be the reason for Christie's sudden disappearance and Archie was quickly propelled to the position of chief suspect. From *The Evening Standard*:

> "For many hours to-day scores of police officers, special constables and civilians vainly searched the mist-enshrouded downs near Guildford, and the well-known Silent Pool and other ponds have been dragged."

The writer's disappearance dominated the British

newspapers for weeks and numerous sightings of her were reported to the police by members of the public from all over the country. Fellow crime novelists Arthur Conan Doyle and Dorothy L. Sayers joined in the hunt. Rumours abounded that Christie had committed suicide or been murdered.

Eleven days later, she was discovered staying at the Swan Hydropathic Hotel in Harrogate, North Yorkshire, under the name of Mrs. Teresa Neele. A banjo player there had recognised her. She had no conclusive explanation as to how she got there and the case even now remains an enigma, long after her death.

Christie was not the only famous name to visit the area. The much celebrated Poet Laureate Alfred, Lord Tennyson was a regular visitor to the Pool according to his son's memoirs. No doubt he enjoyed the spot's inspirational serenity.

Perhaps the area's eerie calm has made it inevitable that a ghost legend would become attached to the place sooner or later. It's certainly not true that the pool is bottomless; in fact it is rather shallow these days, and (of course) birds do sing in the trees as they sing in any others. In fact, wildlife is abundant here. Birds peck among the leaves and stones of the snaking pathway before skipping lightly into the underbrush as you approach. Frogs croak along the waters' edge. Insects buzz amid the foliage.

Even the Pool's famously clear waters are not caused by any supernatural effect. Thanks to being spring-fed from underground water that has passed through chalk deposits (the Pool is thought to be the remains of an ancient quarry), the water carries no sediment to cloud its depths. Sometimes small bubbles can be seen at the Pool's far end as the spring waters come up through the rock.

Certainly, though, the Silent Pool is enchanting with or without the stories that have become associated with it.

Sadly, in recent years it has come under attack by the invasive weed Crassula helmsii. This weed is also known as the New Zealand Pigmy Weed or Australian Swamp

Stonecrop and it out-competes native flora and forms dense layers that choke the waters of much-needed light and oxygen.

The weed is thought to have been introduced to the Pool by someone carelessly tipping the contents of an unwanted aquarium into it. If it had been allowed to grow unchecked, it would have changed the Silent Pool and Sherbourne Pond drastically, "leaving nothing but a green spongy mass, devoid of life". Thankfully, the sum of £50,000 was recently raised and work is currently underway to eradicate the weed and restore the waters to their former glory.

Another success story found locally comes in the form of Silent Pool Rosé, a young wine from the Albury Organic Vineyard that lies next to the Pool. It has already received high praise and won multiple awards, even being chosen to be served on board the Royal Barge during the celebrations that marked Queen Elizabeth's Diamond Jubilee in 2012. And so it seems, by pure coincidence, that the tragic story of Emma and her encounter with the King comes full circle with the Silent Pool and a Queen—this time, thankfully, with far nicer consequences.

9
Wymering Manor

Phantom hands, bloody nuns and playful spirit children.

On the face of it, Wymering Manor appears to be the quintessential English haunted house. It has everything: a long and colourful history, a generous helping of spectral nuns, an old legend, ghostly youngsters who scamper about on the upper floors, poltergeist activity and even the phantom of an embalmed girl. Still more startling are the reports that come from the Panelled Room where phantom hands, dreams of death and oppressive atmospheres have terrified people over the years.

Almost certainly the oldest house in the UK's only island city, Portsmouth, Wymering Manor has an uncertain future despite its impressive provenance. Built upon land that was once owned by Edward the Confessor and then William the Conqueror after him, archaeological studies have found that the surrounding area has been inhabited since at least the time of the Roman occupation of Britain. The Manor itself is thought to incorporate Saxon and Roman building materials, but most of it is of Tudor construction, dating back to the 1500s.

During its existence, the building has been used to

garrison armed forces, as a monastery, a vicarage and a plain old private residence—although, a rather grand one at that. In 1959 it survived a demolition order and was converted into a youth hostel. Now though, the Manor stands empty—well, empty of the *living* anyway. According to *The Daily Mail* newspaper, not even the security guards hang around for long, as they categorically refuse to work night shifts.

Thanks to its reputation for being haunted, the Manor has become an attractive destination for paranormal investigation teams nationwide, and many groups have claimed to experience things like light anomalies, objects moving by themselves, the ubiquitous temperature drops that seem to go hand-in-hand with haunted houses, interesting EVPs and even full-blown apparitions.

The unnerving sounds of children laughing and whispering on the upper floors have also been heard from time to time. Strange figures have been spotted in windows and the ghost of an embalmed girl wanders the Manor's many rooms. This girl, named Elizabeth, had the misfortune to die during the social season. Not wanting a little thing like death to get in the way, her family decided that it would be prudent if they postponed their mourning until the season's close. To this end they had Elizabeth embalmed and her face painted to look as it did in life. No wonder her unhappy spirit is linked with the Manor still. Elizabeth's portrait is often said to still hang somewhere in the Manor's interior. Sadly, pinning down details for this strange story is difficult. Despite what most sources for this story say, no painting of Elizabeth hangs in the Manor. The nearest similar portrait would be one that belonged to one-time owner Thomas Parr which depicted a family member of his—a child. Furthermore, no records exist of an embalmed corpse. Janet Hird, on behalf of the Friends of Old Wymering tells me that this story might be related to the local tale of a girl who now rests in Wymering Churchyard. Her name was Elizabeth Harrison and she died in 1772 after being shot dead somewhere nearby. Her epitaph reads:

All you my Friends who this Way passeth by,
Observe the adjacent field there shot was I:
In Bloom of Youth I had no thought of Death,
So sudden was I forced to yield my breath,
Therefore I'd have you to prepare your way,
For Heav'ns high summons all men must obey.

Conjecture points to her lover, the son of a local farmer, as being the murderer. The story ends with him being hanged from a tree somewhere near to the scene of her death.

In 2004, members of the Hampshire Ghost Club managed to discover the possible identity of one of the Manor's many ghosts as being Sir Francis Austen. Austen, the brother of the distinguished novelist Jane Austen, was at one time the churchwarden of the nearby Wymering Parish Church, so perhaps that is why his spirit is to be found lingering at the Manor. For most of his life, though, he had been a naval officer of some merit, serving with Lord Nelson and rising to the lofty rank of Admiral of the Fleet. Is Austen also the 'Victorian man' in black clothing and a hat who has been seen in the dining room and grounds?

Owners

While evidence of a Roman settlement around Wymering survives, it appears that the area was named after a later personality—a prominent Saxon fellow called Wimm. Sometime after Wimm, it became the home of William Mauduit, a Norman knight who (probably) aided William the Conqueror's invasion in 1066 and was gifted the land in return for his military service. It seems that Mauduit owned quite a lot of land here and there. He got a local girl called Hawyse pregnant and she bore him a son called Robert. They married the next year and had two more boys together, whom they named Thomas and

William.

After Mauduit's ownership, as you'd expect, many distinguished families called Wymering Manor home (or at least owned the estate). Testing by Dr. Martin Bridge and the Oxford Dendrochronology Laboratory indicated with some accuracy that the wood used to build the original part of the present house was cut down in 1581 proving that parts of the existing house were older than first thought.

In the mid-1800s, the colourful Reverend George Nugee became Wymering's vicar and bought the Manor to have as his rectory. He held at least one large festival in the grounds to which he invited everyone from the neighbouring area to come along and enjoy shows, awards and games. Some two thousand locals attended. At one point he played host to Queen Emma of the Sandwich Isles. Over the years, he added a chapel and refectory before eventually resigning and moving along the coast to settle in Devon.

In 1873, the Manor was taken on by a local farmer and landowner called George Peel. Then, Lady Fleetwood and her nephew Thomas Knowlys Parr moved in. Parr, who some thought a descendant of Katherine Parr, one of Henry VIII's six wives, was well-liked in the area for his benevolent nature. He experienced quite a few strange things during his time at Wymering, foremost of which was his encounter with a 'violet lady'.

The story goes that one night, a ghost clad in a long, flowing violet dress appeared at the end of Thomas Parr's bed, waking him. He recognised the vision as being a cousin of his that had died some years before in 1917. When the spirit spoke it told him about matters of religion and family. It ended the strange visit by saying "Well, Tommy dear, I must leave you now as we are waiting to receive Aunt Em."

Parr found out the following morning that 'Aunt Em' had died that very night.

Another relation of Thomas Parr's was involved in a

paranormal encounter in the Blue Room. She stayed overnight and locked her door with care, fearful as she was of burglars, only to wake the next morning and find her door had somehow been silently unlocked and flung open. Thomas changed some sections of the house, adding the two Jacobean-style staircases that frame the hallway and many items of furniture. Perhaps it was this remodelling that disturbed dormant ghosts. He died on the 5th of June, 1938.

World War Two saw the Manor taken over by the armed forces to be used by an "anti-aircraft unit and [a] chemical warfare unit", with military personnel being billeted in the house and grounds and the Home Guard using it to train. After the Allies were victorious the Manor was sold to Mr. Day, (his first name proves elusive) a local builder, who built houses on some of the grounds and then sold on the rest to Leonard Metcalfe, an engineer and inventor.

Together with his wife Marion, Leonard Metcalfe set about undoing the damage caused by military use, which included graffiti left behind by some of the soldiers. Like Thomas Knowlys Parr before him, he had a variety of close encounters with his house's ghostly guests. One regular sighting was the choir of nuns from the Sisterhood of St Mary the Virgin who would walk across the hall at midnight, singing softly. In life, the nuns had visited the house in the mid-1800s, but why they would leave a spectral impression is anyone's guess. Perhaps they linger due to the other nun that, according to writer Stephen Wagner, has been sighted looking down the attic staircase, her hands dripping with crimson blood.

Leonard Metcalfe also encountered one of the creepiest phenomena boasted by the Manor. In the Panelled Room, which was a bedroom at the time, he was completing his ablutions when he felt a disembodied hand on his shoulder. Spinning on his heel, he saw nothing out of place. Metcalfe's wife and mother (and many others since) often reported feeling an oppressive atmosphere pervading this room. They even sensed that there was some kind of presence there and that the walls would feel like they were 'closing in' around them. Children's laughter has also been heard here as have "shrieks of terror" during the night.

Night time in the Panelled Room also brings the possibility of another terror.

One person to sleep in the room experienced a vivid dream in which they saw a man hanging from a particular tree in the Manor's grounds. The morning brought the discovery that the dream had come true and a man had indeed hanged himself in the night. Since then, more people have reported similar dreams.

On a related note, until the mid-1750s, a gallows for hanging those disreputable highwaymen that plagued local roads used to exist at the south-western edge of the Manor's land. Skeletons were discovered under the floor of the building that had been constructed over the 'Wymering Gibbet'.

Wymering Manor is also home to an interesting old legend. Sir Roderick of Portchester—or 'Reckless Roddy' as he was also known—was a nefarious young buck who paid a visit to the Manor in an attempt to seduce the newly married girl there. Her husband had been called away and Roderick had decided to try his luck. All was not to go in the philanderer's favour though as, without warning, the husband returned and caught Roderick who promptly ran to his horse meaning to flee. The husband shot him dead. It is said that even today, when newlyweds stay at the Manor, the sounds of a spectral horse's hooves can be heard in the early morning hours. This was an added phenomenon supposedly witnessed by Leonard Metcalfe.

Another old legend concerns the existence of some hidden passageways beneath the house. There is thought to be a tunnel—or a series of tunnels—connecting Wymering Manor to Wymering Parish Church, maybe even continuing on three miles further to reach Southwick Priory to the north. This tunnel is most likely to be an old kitchen drain running from the house. No tunnels were uncovered during nearby digging by electrical and water companies.

After Leonard Metcalfe passed away, the building was slated for demolition. It was saved only when Portsmouth City Council stepped in, selling off some of the garden for redevelopment and then leasing the main buildings to the Youth Hostels Association in 1960.

The paranormal activity carried on under the management of the YHA, with more reports of horse's hooves crunching on the lane and further weird goings-on in the Panelled Room. And it was during the YHA's time at the Manor that it became a favourite destination for ghost hunters from across the UK. In fact, the unverified reports of encounters at Wymering Manor are legion during this time. The ghost of a Victorian lady named Miss Emiline Nightingale was seen peering out of windows and generally walking about before vanishing into a wall where once there was a doorway. Spirit animals were sensed or seen; as was a young girl, around ten years old and wearing a green dress; a faceless suicide; an enigmatic man in a cowboy hat; and a crying baby—heard but never seen. Lights and taps flicked on by themselves and shrouded figures flitted amongst the shadows.

Ghost hunters with *Spooky Locations* attest to the location's high levels of paranormal activity, and said this of Wymering Manor: "We can quite honestly say that it is one of the most haunted places we have ever been in; plenty of photos were taken whilst there, capturing some unexplained images along with plenty of light anomalies. One of our members was even slapped across the chest!"

The Youth Hostel Association's occupation of the Manor came to an end in 2005 when a 'structural collapse' meant the building was unsafe.

Once again, the Manor's survival was under threat and so a group called the Friends of Old Wymering was formed to help protect it. The Manor was put up for sale by auction three times in 2010, but failed to sell because of the cost necessary to restore and make safe the structure.

So, while economic spectres hang bleakly over Wymering Manor, are the spiritual spectres inside just as real?

Well, the short answer is: *it's very hard to tell*. While the sheer number of anecdotes suggest that something might be going on there, what that something might be is rather hard to say. Certainly, the Manor's long history lends itself to tales of ghosts and ghouls and if a tunnel did exist at some point, others point to the possibility that, like we saw in the earlier chapter about Dunwich, smugglers using it might have intentionally spread rumours to keep people away. Wymering is close to the sea, after all, and smuggling took place all over the South Coast. But this is pure conjecture and even if it was proven it doesn't explain the findings of more recent years. *The Daily Mail's* claim that security guards refuse to work there at night is certainly not true, though.

Visitors have said that in spite of the unearthly denizens, the building does seem to have a friendly atmosphere about it, and for sure, it would be a great loss to the area if demolition lay in the Manor's future.

For those that wish to enquire about Wymering Manor's prospects, or offer aid to help secure its future, please contact the Friends of Old Wymering.

10
The Croglin Vampire

Britain's oldest vampire attack?.

The quiet Cumbrian hamlet of Croglin is a cosy place. It is to be found in the picturesque Lake District, settled in between the long, low mountains of the Pennines and the snaking 90-mile-long River Eden. But this is Britain, and even in a peaceful setting like this, the mysterious and macabre can lurk around any corner. In fact, Croglin claims ownership of one of the country's rare unexplained legends—one that tells of a vampire.

While some retellings of the Croglin Vampire story disagree on minor points, the version by Augustus Hare is the best known and, on the face of it at least, definitive. Augustus John Hare was a popular high society raconteur during the mid-to-late 1800s. His version of the Croglin Vampire was published under the title *The Beast of Croglin Grange* in his six-volume autobiography *The Story of My Life*. He claimed to have heard it first at the wedding of one of his relatives, a Lady Victoria Liddel, daughter of Henry Thomas Liddell, 1st Earl of Ravensworth. She was marrying a British Army captain named Edward Rowe Fisher-Rowe (who, as a young lieutenant had taken part of the Charge of the Heavy Brigade at Balaclava) and it was he that told Hare the story on the 29th of July, 1874. It is tempting to reproduce Hare's version in all its glory here, but an abridged edition will have to suffice:

"Captain Fisher told us this really extraordinary story connected with his own family:

"[The Fisher] family is of very ancient lineage, and for many hundreds of years they have possessed a very curious sort of place in Cumberland, which bears the weird name of Croglin Grange. The great characteristic of the house is that never at any period of its very long existence has it been more than one storey high, but it has a terrace from which large grounds sweep away towards the Church in the hollow, and a fine distant view.

"When the Fishers outgrew Croglin Grange in family and fortune, they went away to the south, and they let Croglin Grange.

"They were extremely fortunate in their tenants, two brothers and a sister. They heard their praises from all quarters.

"The winter was spent most happily by the new inmates of Croglin Grange, who shared in all the little social pleasures of the district, and made themselves very popular."

One night during the summer, after a long day enjoying the countryside, the three siblings all went wearily to their beds. Despite the heat, the sister closed her window and sat up in bed, watching "the marvellous beauty of that summer night". Soon, however, a strange set of lights came into view. They were a pair and they disappeared and reappeared as they travelled behind tree trunks and walls, approaching inexorably. As they grew closer, she was able to discern that they belonged to a ghastly figure!

> "As she watched it, the most uncontrollable horror seized her. She longed to scream, but her voice seemed paralysed, her tongue glued to the roof of her mouth.
>
> "Immediately she jumped out of bed and rushed to the door, but as she was unlocking it, she heard scratch, scratch, scratch upon the window, and saw a hideous brown face with flaming eyes glaring in at her. She rushed back to the bed, but the creature continued to scratch, scratch, scratch on the window. Suddenly the scratching sound ceased. And a kind of pecking sound took its place. Then, in her agony, she became aware that the creature was unpicking the lead! The noise continued, and a diamond pane of glass fell into the room. Then a long bony finger of the creature came in and turned the handle of the window, and the window opened, and the creature came in; and it came across the room, and her terror was so great that she could not scream, and it came up to the bed and twisted its long bony fingers in her hair, and it dragged her head over the side of the bed, and—it bit her violently in the throat."

Woken by the noise, the two brothers rushed to their sister's aid. The lock on her bedroom door was smashed using a metal poker and the two men stormed into the room. A terrible sight confronted them. Blood, starkly scarlet, was flowing from their sister's neck wound and she lay quiet and pale on her bed. The creature had fled the way he had come in, still visible through the window as it strode into the murk of night in the direction of the churchyard. Anxious for her life, the brothers tended to their sister but soon she seemed mostly recovered.

The initial hypothesis was that the attacker had been a lunatic, escaped from an asylum somewhere. After the local doctor advised that she must have "a change, mental and physical", the trio went to Switzerland where they flourished.

Eventually, a yearning for England brought them back to those shores and once more they were living at Croglin Grange. No alterations were made to the Grange—the opinion amongst them being that they would be very unlucky to encounter another escaped madman. However, the brothers' precautions did include keeping pistols loaded in their rooms at night, just in case something happened. And, as Hare tells us, something did happen.

> "The winter passed most peacefully and happily. In the following March the sister was suddenly awakened by a sound she remembered only too well—scratch, scratch, scratch upon the window, and looking up, she saw, climbed up to the topmost pane of the window, the same hideous brown shrivelled face, with glaring eyes, looking in at her. This time she screamed as loud as she could. Her brothers rushed out of their room with pistols, and out of the front door. The creature was already scudding away across the lawn. One of the brothers fired and hit it in the leg, but still with the other leg it continued to make way, scrambled over the wall into the churchyard, and seemed to disappear into a vault which belonged to a family long extinct.
>
> "The next day the brothers summoned all the tenants of Croglin Grange, and in their presence the vault was opened. A horrible scene revealed itself. The vault was full of coffins; they had been broken open, and their contents, horribly mangled and distorted,

were scattered over the floor. One coffin alone remained intact. Of that the lid had been lifted, but still lay loose upon the coffin. They raised it, and there, brown, withered, shrivelled, mummified, but quite entire, was the same hideous figure which had looked in at the windows of Croglin Grange, with the marks of a recent pistol shot in the leg; and they did the only thing that can lay a vampire—they burnt it."

While Hare was celebrated for his many biographies and what might be called 'travel logs' today, he was also famed for his love of ghost stories and his skill (as is evident from the passage above in retelling them was uncommon).

But does Hare's version deserve to be called definitive? Anthony Hogg's excellent blog *Diary of an Amateur Vampirologist* offers a degree of corroboration for Hare's version via one of the writer's contemporaries: a man called Clifford Harrison. Harrison said of Hare's ghostly tales that "they are all labelled and certified with names, dates and references—the most authenticated and documented ghosts I know." Harrison offered further support by saying: "I have heard the tale also from a descendent of the possessors of Crogley [sic] Grange, in which house the grisly incident occurred, and the tale is undoubtedly full of curious and somewhat unanswerable questions." Hare certainly seems to have relished telling and retelling the story of the Croglin Vampire as references to it appear in a variety of places in the late 1800s.

However, there are a few problems with both Hare's version and those provided by others. Firstly, the "pistol shot" dug out from the dead vampire's leg, and the fact that it is directly referred to as a lead ball in some accounts means that the pistols used by the brothers were probably flintlocks or, at a push, used the percussion cap system, and were supposedly bought in Switzerland. If personal defence was the aim, these would be bizarre weapons to purchase as at the time the story took place hinted by Hare to be the mid-1800s (and by another writer called Valentine Dyall to be even later: "the Cumberland phenomenon can be definitely placed in the years 1875-76") because breech-loading metallic cartridges and the Minié ball had helped to make long-lived lead ball ammunition utterly obsolete—even more so if the pistols were flintlocks which had been superseded decades before.

Secondly, as Charles G. Harper pointed out in *Haunted Houses*, the Croglin Grange of the story seemed to never have existed:

> "It is to be added, from personal observation, that there is no place styled Croglin Grange. There are Croglin High Hall and Low Hall. Both are farm-houses, very like one another, and not in any particulars resembling the description given. Croglin Low Hall is probably the house indicated, but it is at least a mile distant from the church, which has been rebuilt. The churchyard contains no tomb which by any stretch of the imagination could be identified with that described by Mr. Hare."

So, with anachronistic details, a dubious location, no church or tomb to act as the vampire's den—was Hare's story a fabrication? Or was it an amalgam of other stories that he had heard or read about on his many travels; stories that when added together make a splendid tale to enthral and entertain an audience, but when analysed with any kind of enthusiasm quickly fall apart?

Supporting the idea that Hare took the Croglin Vampire story from sources other than real-life fact was D. Scott Rogo's research for *Fate* Magazine. Rogo was a writer and researcher of all things parapsychological. He noticed the many similarities between the Croglin Vampire case and a section of that popular 'penny dreadful' by James Malcolm Rymer, *Varney the Vampire; or, The Feast of Blood*. '*Varney*' was first made available to the public in 1845-47 as a series of pamphlets before being published as a (very long) book, and its opening chapters seem to bear a suspiciously close resemblance to Hare's account of the foreboding goings-on at Croglin Grange.

There is the "girl young and beautiful as a spring morning" asleep in her old house when, out of a terrible storm there appears a "figure tall and gaunt, endeavouring from the outside to unclasp the window". The fearsome fellow's long finger nails search the glass for ingress and, finding it, he enters the petrified girl's chamber where he seizes her neck "in his fang-like teeth—a gush of blood, and a hideous sucking noise follows". Her screams wake the young men of the house who rush to her aid, one discharging a pistol into the hastily retreating vampire as it disappears into the night.

It bears an undeniable similarity to the Croglin story, so, understandably, Rogo quickly concluded that the Croglin Vampire could only have come from *Varney the Vampire*. Had Hare's love of thrilling an audience led him to plagiarism?

Francis Fabian Clive-Ross was a publisher and author whose works focused on occultism. He visited Croglin on a number of occasions from November 1962 onwards and talked extensively to the local residents about the vampire legend. Where Charles Harper had concluded that Croglin Grange couldn't have existed as it had in the story, dismissing Croglin Low Hall as ill-fitting with no appropriate churchyard or tomb; Clive-Ross discovered that Croglin Low Hall was in fact a very likely candidate for the Grange and a small chapel had indeed existed near the house at one time. This chapel had been at first damaged and then later demolished entirely sometime during Oliver Cromwell's years in power (1653-1658), with the stones later taken away for reuse. In fact, its foundation stones—though overgrown by flora—were still visible.

More interesting developments would come thanks to the knowledge of a local woman named Mrs. Dorothy Parkin who lived at Ainstable in a house called Slack Cottage. She held the key to unlocking many of the story's mysteries, and through her, Clive-Ross found out that until about 1720 "According to the deeds of Croglin Low Hall, it was commonly called Croglin Grange." Not only that, but Croglin Low Hall still retained somewhat incongruous stone corbels that looked as though they had supported a roof at one time, meaning the structure could conceivably have been only a single storey high at some point in its existence. Suddenly, it appeared as though the story's likely location was verified.

It turned out that Mrs. Parkin's late husband, the cricket-loving Inglewood Urban Parkin, had actually owned Croglin Low Hall at one point, so she had more vital knowledge to aid Clive-Ross' search for truth. She even claimed to have personally known a male descendant of the Fisher family. This gentleman was born in the 1860s and had known the story since a very early age, having been told about it by his grandparents. This snippet of information, if true, would help to push back the Croglin Vampire story from a time post-*Varney the Vampire*, to the late 1600s—two centuries earlier. It would also remove any possibility of Augustus Hare having copied the penny dreadful by James Malcolm Rymer.

Additionally, this earlier date meant that the brothers' use of lead ball ammunition and flintlock pistols was suddenly quite appropriate for the time.

To be frank, would Hare really have risked his reputation as a raconteur by plagiarising a penny dreadful from only a few decades earlier? This is especially doubtful when you consider that *Varney the Vampire* must have been fairly well-known in the capital at least and so any similarities detected immediately. This leaves us with the curious question of how Hare got the date so wrong.

Perhaps the inaccurate date was due to the undoubtedly copious amounts of alcohol that must have flowed at Captain Fisher-Rowe's wedding...

Clive-Ross' excellent research also unearthed a new variation on the legend, with a second victim being brought to light, this time a young child:

> "Another tradition connected with the vampire involves Croglin Low Hall, and the two stories were generally repeated together. This story relates that at the time the tenants there had a three-year-old child. From being a happy, healthy child she became frightened, sickly and pale, and the parents noticed what they thought were rat's teeth marks on her throat. After Miss Cranswell had been attacked new light was thrown on the child's plight, and the father was one of those who took part in the laying of the vampire."

In some versions of the Croglin Vampire story the brothers and their sister are given names: Amelia, Edward and William Cranswell, newly arrived to Britain's shores from Australia where their father had made his fortune. The accuracy of these names and the thought that the Cranswells were 'outsiders' is (or was, at least) supported by local knowledge. This is very interesting considering that the origin of these names seems to be Valentine Dyall's book *Unexplained Mysteries*. Augustus Hare himself never named the tenants of Croglin Grange and there appear to be no records verifying the existence of any Cranswells living in the area. The precision of the 'Croglin Hall Vampire' chapter of Dyall's book has been brought into question in other regards as well, with it containing much "additional information, mostly without any stated authority" and "nuggets not found in *any* previous version of the story". So, where Dyall dug up the Cranswells' identities from is anybody's guess, although certainly his version has influenced some of the residents of Croglin itself and, as one writer has put it, "seeped into local knowledge".

So, if not the Cranswells, who could the tenants have been? If the rough date of the late 1600s is to be believed it might have been a family called the Towrys. Records show that George Towry possessed the Grange in 1688, with it remaining in his family's ownership until the death of the last of their line, William Towry, in 1727. Sadly, any connection the Towrys might have had with vampirism has not been preserved.

Aside from the veracity of the minutiae of the story, could there be a rational explanation for the so-called vampire? Two more investigators, Lionel and Patricia Fanthorpe, certainly seem to think so. In their *Big Book of Mysteries* they give us an intriguing hypothesis to consider:

> "When we were lecturing on the Croglin vampire phenomenon in the 1970s, an ingenious young medical practitioner in the audience put forward a fascinating—and totally rational—theory. He suggested that there was nothing paranormal about the case: Amelia was attacked by someone mentally ill who had, as part of that mental illness, made a den or hiding place among the tombs surrounding the derelict church adjacent to Croglin Low Hall. After Edward shot him in the leg, the psychopath retreated to the vault where he had been living for some time.
>
> "The 'vampire' gets a sudden bright idea. [...] The psychopath extracts the green lead pistol ball from the wound in his leg. He smears fresh red blood from that same leg wound onto the mouth and hands of the long-dead corpse. He takes the Swiss lead pistol ball that he has prised from the deep flesh wound on his injured leg and thrusts it

into the dried parchment-like flesh of the long-dead occupant of the coffin on the central dais. The psychopath sneaks silently out and puts as much distance as he can between himself and Croglin."

After fleeing from Croglin, it is suggested that the attacker died of blood loss, shock or perhaps gangrene, far from Croglin and any possible suspicion that he might be a vampire. Of course, from then on, there would have been no more attacks at Croglin Grange and the local vampire slayers would have considered their work to have been effective. It's undoubtedly an attractive and wholly possible idea. Couple it with local superstition and the embellishments of successive story-tellers and suddenly the random attacks of a desperate or mentally ill person take on an altogether more macabre and otherworldly hue. The only possible hiccup to this theory is that the attacker needed to have known his pursuers thought him to be a vampire. Otherwise, why would he have known that placing the bullet from his wound into a dried up corpse would get him off the hook?

Thanks to its age, it's hard to imagine the Croglin Vampire legend ever being truly verified. Without doubt, any version of the story that survives today is assuredly a twisted and misshapen adaptation of whatever form the original took. Even if Hare's account was utterly accurate it still remains that his source's knowledge was passed down through family members orally—a method which, of course, is at the whim of exaggeration and forgetfulness. Regardless, the story has become a classic tale of spindly vampirism; chilling and eerie, and its tenets have echoed quietly through blood-sucking fiction for centuries. So now, when retiring to bed, make sure you listen out for a gentle picking at your window, for it could be the Vampire of Croglin Grange looking for an evening tipple...

GLOSSARY

The descriptions here have been kept brief wherever possible, so for in-depth elucidations I suggest independent research. This glossary is also by no means complete, and meant to act only as a guide for readers of this book.

Anomaly
A broad, umbrella term for anything that deviates from what might have been expected to happen. *Anomaly* is often used as a neutral expression, in comparison to more loaded words like 'supernatural' or 'paranormal'.

Apparition
The visible manifestation of a spirit.
See *Ghost*
See *Haunting*

Apport
The movement or materialisation of an object that takes place seemingly without human assistance.

Automatic Writing
Writing that is purported to be produced outside of the writer's control. Sometimes referred to as *'psychography'*.

Channelling
Channelling is the name given to the process of a spirit communicating to an audience via a medium. The medium is said to 'channel' the spirit.

Clairaudience
A skill supposedly possessed by some mediums. It gives them the ability to hear sounds and voices that are said to come from the spirit world or other supernatural sources.

Clairvoyance

The ability of a medium to see a spirit or image either in their 'mind's eye', or as a projection in front of them. Taken from the French *'clair'* meaning 'clear' and *'voyance'* meaning 'vision'. The terms clairvoyance and clairaudience are sometimes grouped together under the name 'clairsentience'.

Cold Reading

A technique employed by magicians, mentalists and bogus mind-readers (amongst others) to convince their audience that they are able to discern personal or otherwise hidden information about them—as if from thin air. Basically, it involves the use of statements that seem to be specific but are in fact very general.

Cold Spot

Usually found inside supposedly haunted buildings, a cold spot is an area of varying size where the temperature is considerably lower than that surrounding it. Not to be confused with a draught.

Crisis Apparition

An image or apparition witnessed when the subject is about to die, or has just died. The crisis apparition usually appears to a loved one.

Dowsing

Dowsers believe that using pendulums, bent metal rods, or forked twigs will help them locate fresh supplies of water, mineral deposits, electrical currents or even lost objects.

Ectoplasm

A substance allegedly produced by a medium during a trance. It can take a variety of shapes, from intangible mists to solid rods. *Ectoplasm* is derived from the Greek words *'ektos'*, meaning 'outside', and *'plasma'*, meaning 'formed'.

Electromagnetic Field
Often shortened to just 'EMF', an electromagnetic field is
produced by electrically charged objects. Depending upon
its strength and frequency, it can have a wide range of
effects upon human beings which is why some people
think that electromagnetic fields are the root cause of
some hauntings or ghost sightings.
See *EMF Detector*

Electronic Voice Phenomenon
Recordings of voices or similar sounds that were not heard
by investigators at the time the recordings took place.
Whether the voices actually belong to spirits or some other
entity is open to interpretation.

Elementals
These are thought to be nature spirits with strong
connections to the four basic elements of earth, fire, air
and water. "Elemental spirits possess supernatural powers
and are usually invisible to humans, living among the trees,
rivers, plants, bogs, mountains, and minerals."—
Wikipedia. Elves, fairies, gnomes and the like.

EMF
See *Electromagnetic Field*

EMF Detector
An electronic, handheld instrument for measuring the
potency and direction of any electromagnetic fields within
its vicinity. Sometimes referred to as a magnetometer or a
gauss meter.
See *Electromagnetic Field*

ESP
See *Extrasensory Perception*

EVP
See *Electronic Voice Phenomenon*

Exorcism
This is the ritualised expulsion of an unwanted spiritual or demonic entity. Exorcisms assume many differing forms across a multitude of religions.

Extrasensory Perception
ESP is a term first used by Frederic Myers, the founder of the SPR. Simply put, it is the capability to sense something without using the 'traditional' five senses of taste, touch, sight, hearing and smell. Also called *'the sixth sense'*.
See *Society for Psychical Research*

Fortean Phenomena
Named after the American writer Charles Fort, this is a term meaning a "general bag of weird phenomena". The UK magazine *Fortean Times* is very popular.

Fraudulent Mediums Act
Introduced in 1951, the Act repealed the out-dated 1735 Witchcraft Act and introduced new legislation for prosecuting those who intended to profit from deceit. Repealed in 2008.

Ghost
The manifestation of a dead person.
See *Haunting*

The Ghost Club
Founded in 1962, the Ghost Club claims to be "the oldest organisation in the world associated with psychical research". Some big names have been members of this non-profit organisation: Charles Dickens, Siegfried Sassoon, Harry Price, Donald Campbell, Peter Cushing, Peter Underwood, Maurice Grosse.

Ghost Lights
Generally; unexplainable bright lights. Might also refer to the folkloric Will-o'-the-wisp.

See *Will-o'-the-wisp*

Grey Lady
See *Ghost*
See *Haunting*
See *Apparition*

Haunting
Put simply, a haunting is a series of unexplained events that occur at a location. There are a great many of these unexplained events, including: the movement of furniture and objects, seemingly by themselves; disembodied footsteps, voices, screams; the presence of incongruous smells; the manifestation of apparitions; and so on. The list is a long one. Of course, not all alleged hauntings are the same and there are even different types of hauntings, categorised thusly:
"Residual: The most common type of haunting; the spirit is either partially or completely unaware of current events or people, but has remained behind for any reason or reasons.
"Recursive: Also known as a pattern haunting, often confused with residual hauntings, these are hauntings that follow a general pattern of events, usually at specific times. These hauntings, like residuals, often reflect the spirit being partially or totally unaware of current events and people.
"Intelligent: These hauntings usually involve interaction with humans, and can be anywhere from friendly and benign to frightening and severely aggressive.
"Possession: Basically, the occupation of a human by a spirit. Not necessarily a haunting, but often confused as one, which is why it's placed in this list."*

Hypnagogic Hallucinations
Vivid images produced as the mind moves into sleep are described as being *Hypnagogic*.
See *Hypnopompic Hallucinations*

Hypnopompic Hallucinations

When moving to wakefulness, the mind passes through the hypnopompic state. Sometimes, especially when the person was experiencing rapid eye movement sleep (in which most dreams are said to take place), dream-like imagery can remain and become dragged into semi-consciousness. This has been proposed as a possible explanation for reports of apparitions, out-of-body experiences and sleep paralysis. The term *hypnagogia* has become a general description for both hypnopompic and hypnagogic states.

See *Hypnagogic Hallucinations*

Ideomotor Effect

The conversion of an 'idea' into 'movement'. This is the theory that suggestion and subconscious thought can have a physical effect on a subject, this effect manifesting as muscular movements. The ideomotor effect has been put forward as a scientific explanation for the movements of dowsing rods and pendulums, Ouija board glasses and planchettes, table tipping and more besides.

Infrasound

Infrasound is sound that is lower in frequency than what humans can normally hear. The lecturer and engineer Vic Tandy researched infrasound and discovered that at some frequencies it was able to affect eyesight and even move inanimate objects. He added that "an infrasonic signal of 19 Hz might be responsible for some ghost sightings and ghost phenomena".

Ley 'Lines'

Some people think leys are straight lines that criss-cross the country, allowing the passage of energy. The existence of these mysterious leys was first suggested in the early 1920s by Alfred Watkins.

Lithobolia
A devil who throws stones.
See *Poltergeist*.

Magnetometer
See *EMF Detector*

Materialization
The physical manifestation of a dead person's spirit. This is said to often take place during a séance when the medium emits ectoplasm so that the spirit can use it to assume a physical form.

Medium
"Often interchangeable with 'psychic', the term implies that the medium acts as an intermediary between worlds, a conduit for messages from the Beyond, a channel for healing powers and so on."**

Misperception
This is surely the most common and rational reason for explaining away supernatural phenomena. The mind often plays tricks on us and, coupled with the power of suggestion and/or a lack of knowledge, is frequently behind reports of paranormal activity—whether those involved know it or not.

Night-Vision Equipment
Designed for use in low light conditions, night-vision can form an important part of a ghost hunter's equipment bag.

Old Hag Syndrome
See *Sleep Paralysis*

Orbs
This is a photographic anomaly, the merits of which are hotly debated. It usually appears as a two dimensional circle of light on digital photographs. Some people claim

to be able to see faces in them, and even believe they are in fact the remnants of a dead person. However, doubters draw upon many arguments to disprove this theory, insisting that orbs are merely dust, water droplets, lens flares and so on.

Ouija Board
A board game that takes its name from the French and German words for *yes*. It features numbers, some words and the letters of the alphabet. The idea is that a spirit would move a glass or planchette to spell out words and thereby communicate with the players. Some people maintain staunchly that the Ouija Board is a dangerous tool—a gateway to demonic forces. Others dismiss it entirely. Whatever the truth, it's rather telling that even to this day it continues to be stocked by shops such as *Toys 'R' Us* and marketed towards children.

Pareidolia
The human mind is programmed to perceive patterns and shapes all around it—and is especially good at recognising facial structure. The example usually offered to illustrate pareidolia is the identification of shapes in cloud formations. Pareidolia is the rationalisation behind why some people see ghosts in some perfectly unsupernatural photographs.
See also *Simulacra*

Paranormal
Something that is beyond what is accepted as scientifically measurable or explainable.

Parapsychology
Parapsychologists study the world of the paranormal. The term tends to be used as a replacement for the older phrase 'psychical research'.

Phantom Hitchhiker
A 'classic' haunting, the phantom hitchhiker seems real enough to be offered a lift by some unsuspecting motorist, only to vanish inexplicably.
 See *Lepke*

Photographic Anomalies
Basically, these are weird things that show up on camera. Some might say they are ghosts, orbs, supernatural mists or demons; others might insist that they are lens flares, dust particles or water droplets.

Planchette
A triangular, wheeled instrument for use with Ouija Boards or automatic writing.

Poltergeist
A troublesome and sometimes powerful entity that typically seems to emanate or be linked to a person (the 'focus'). Poltergeist cases have been reported for many centuries in many countries. As with most of these things, theories about what they actually are abound. Famous cases include the Black Monk of Pontefract and the Rosenheim Poltergeist.

Possession
The 'invasion' of a person by a spirit or demon.
See *Exorcism*

Precognition
The ability to see into the future.

Preternatural
Things that are unusual or appearing miraculous yet have natural or rational explanations.

Psychic
There are a multitude of types of psychic, but generally, a

psychic is someone who possesses extrasensory perception of some kind.

Psychical Research

An older name that refers to the study of all things that go bump in the night.
See *Parapsychology*

Psychography

See *Automatic Writing*

Psychokinesis

The ability to cause an object to move without physically touching it.

Psychometry

The ability to discern hidden information simply by touching an object related to the information.

Rapping

Banging and knocking noises that are associated with hauntings and poltergeist cases.

Remote Viewing

To see or sense an object or person from afar using the mind.

Séance

A (usually) small gathering of people who use various techniques to attempt to contact the dead.

Simulacra

Objects (and more) that, purely by chance, have the appearance of something else. For example, toast that looks like it has a picture of the Virgin Mary burnt into it.
See also *Pareidolia*

Sleep Paralysis
Sometimes called Old Hag Syndrome, sleep paralysis can take hold either when falling asleep and entering into REM sleep or when waking up. It can be accompanied by quite vivid hallucinations.
See *Hypnopompic Hallucinations*

Society for Psychical Research
Commonly abbreviated to SPR, the Society was formed in with the intention of "learning more about events and abilities commonly described as 'psychic' or 'paranormal' by supporting research, sharing information and encouraging debate."***

Spirit Photography
The image of a spirit captured on camera. Spirit photography flourished in the late Victorian era thanks in part to the popular use of the double exposure.

SPR
See *Society for Psychical Research*

Stone Tape Theory
This is an interesting explanation for some types of hauntings. The theory is that the materials that comprise the building are somehow capable of recording the image of a person or even an event. Some trigger then causes this recording to be played back.

Supernatural
Beyond what is accepted or explained by science (or 'nature').

Synchronicity
A coincidence that seems to be meaningful in some way.

Urban Myths
Urban myths are essentially made-up stories that are

passed around friends, colleagues and relatives. Sometimes their origins lie in fact, although any kernel of truth that might have been part of the original story has long been obscured. More often than not they are pure fiction.

Vigil
Usually held at night, vigils can form part of the ghost hunter's investigative process. It involves staying up through the night and quietly observing a supposedly haunted property.

White Lady
See *Ghost*
See *Haunting*
See *Apparition*

Will-o'-the-Wisp
The mysterious Will-o'-the-wisp is, according to folklore, a phantom light seen by travellers. It is said to lure the unwary into dangerous ground such as swamps or bogs. Also known by many other colourful names, including jack-o'-lantern, hinkypunk and hobby lantern.

*From Scottish-Paranormal.co.uk
**From ASSAP.ac.uk
***From the Society for Psychical Research

RECOMMENDED READING AND SOURCES

As with the first *Eerie Britain* book's recommended reading section, the following entries are those which have either served as inspiring reads or provided source material for this work. Exact source annotation is not included in the main text as an attempt to keep this book more of a 'light read' than an academic text.

Peter Underwood, *The A-Z of British Ghosts*, Chancellor Press, 1992.
Peter Underwood, *This Haunted Isle*, Brockhampton Press, 1998.
Multiple authors, *Great Britain*, Lonely Planet Publications Pty Ltd, 2011.
Bill Eglon Shaw, *Frank Meadow Sutcliffe: A Second Selection*, The Sutcliffe Gallery, 1985.
Michael Shaw, *Frank Meadow Sutcliffe: A Third Selection*, The Sutcliffe Gallery, 1990.
Jan-Andrew Henderson, *The Town Below the Ground*, Mainstream Publishing Company (Edinburgh) Ltd, 2007.
Simon Marsden, *The Journal of a Ghosthunter*, Little, Brown and Company, 1994.
Antony D. Hippisley Coxe, *Haunted Britain*, Pan Books, 1975.
Michael J. Hallowell and Darren W. Ritson, *The Haunting of Willington Mill*, The History Press Ltd, 2011.
Leonard R.N. Ashley, *The complete Book of Devils and Demons*, Barricade Books Inc, 1996.
Tom Slemen, *Haunted Liverpool 13*, The Bluecoat Press, 2006.
Sir Christopher Frayling, *Nightmare: The Birth of Horror*, BBC Books, 1996.
Jessie Adelaide Middleton, *Grey Ghost Book*, E. Nash, 1915.
Malcolm Day, *Ghosts (Amazing and Extraordinary Facts)*, David & Charles, 2011.
Paul McDermott, *The Whitby Ghost Book*, Anderson, 1987.

Jimmie E. Cain Jr., *Bram Stoker and Russophobia: Evidence of the British Fear of Russia in Dracula and The Lady of the Shroud*, McFarland & Company Inc, 2006.

Elizabeth Miller, *Bram Stoker's Dracula: A Documentary Journey into Vampire Country and the Dracula Phenomenon*, Pegasus, 2009.

Lionel and Patricia Fanthorpe, *The Big Book of Mysteries*, Dundurn, 2010.

Charles G. Harper, *Haunted Houses: Tales of the Supernatural with some Accounts of Hereditary Curses and Family Legends*, Chapman & Hall, 1907.

Richard Jones, *Haunted Britain and Ireland*, New Holland, 2001.

Richard Jones, *Haunted London*, New Holland, 2004.

Geoff Holder, *Haunted St Andrews*, The History Press, 2012.

Paul Adams, Eddie Brazil and Peter Underwood, *Shadows in the Nave*, The History Press, 2011.

Vic Tandy and Tony R. Lawrence, *The Ghost in the Machine*, Journal of the Society for Psychical Research, 1998.

Edwin Sidney Hartland, *English Fairy and Folk Tales*, The Walter Scott Publishing Company, 1905(?).

Jeff Belanger, *World's Most Haunted Places: From the Secret Files of Ghostville.Com*, New Page Books, 2005.

Steve Roud, *Superstitions of the British Isles*, Index Books, 2005.

Steve Roud, *London Lore: The Legends and Traditions of the World's Most Vibrant City*, Random House Books, 2008.

John Briggs, Christopher Harrison, Angus McInnes, David Vincent, *Crime and Punishment in England, 1100-1990: An Introductory History*, Palgrave Macmillan, 1996.

Richard Jones, *Haunted Houses of Britain and Ireland*, New Holland, 2005.

Roy Harley Lewis, *Ghosts, Hauntings and the Supernatural World*, David & Charles, 1991.

Rosemary Ellen Guiley, *The Encyclopaedia of Ghosts and Spirits*, Guinness Publishing, 1992.

Karen Farrington, *Hamlyn History – Supernatural*, Hamlyn,

1997.
Charles Dickens, *A Dictionary of London, 1879*, Howard Baker Press, 1879.
Multiple authors, *The Rough Guide to Britain*, Rough Guides Ltd, 2012.
Rory Muir, *Britain and the Defeat of Napoleon, 1807-1815*, Yale University Press, 1996.

Some of the chapter on Wymering Manor is sourced from the guide book *Wymering Manor, a Brief History* which was produced by the Friends of Old Wymering.

Ghost Voices Magazine, bi-monthly, Dragoon Publishing. (Now discontinued.)

WEB

MysteryMag.com UKMythology.co.uk
UKMythology.co.uk ParanormalDatabase.com
PhenomenaMagazine.co.uk SpookyIsles.com
TheWhitbySeagull.co.uk DOAAV.Blogspot.co.uk
MysteriousBritain.co.uk Unexplained-Mysteries.com
ForteanTimes.com GhostClub.org.uk
ParanormalDatabase.com SPR.ac.uk Randi.org
RichardWiseman.Wordpress.com Historic-UK.com
FriendsOfOldWymering.org.uk WhitbyGazette.co.uk
NLPI.co.uk Lionel-Fanthorpe.com DeathGonk.com

The chapters regarding Samlesbury Hall and the Silent Pool were first published in Environmental Graffiti. They appear here in updated, rewritten forms.

Line art drawing of a skull and crossbones courtesy of Pearson Scott Foresman.

THANKS

I am indebted to the following people for lending me their help, time and knowledge. Nick Wenman at Albury Organic Vineyard, Karl Hansell at the Whitby Gazette, Ed Maggs at Maggs Bros. Ltd, Nic Roper, Mickey Gocool from North London Paranormal Investigations for his knowledge of Highgate's various horrors, Martin Cramp from Spooky Locations for help with Wymering Manor, Carly Adams, Graham Preston, Nathan Miles, Christiane Kroebel from Whitby Museum, Patricia & Lionel Fanthorpe for kindly granting me permission to quote their work, Christine Hughes for brilliance in researching the Skirrid Inn's past, Janet Hird on behalf of the Friends of Old Wymering for aid with the none-paranormal aspects of that chapter, Becky for being Becky, Mum & Dad for research, proofreading, encouragement and for giving me my love for spooky stories in the first place, Gerry over in Australia, Katy for her patience, Isabella for spurring me on, Tracy and Warren King, Sharon Jones at Samlesbury Hall, and Hannah Barnett for introducing me to the delights of the Silent Pool.

If you would like to contact the author of this book, then please do so at the following email address, adding 'Eerie Britain 2' to the subject box:

MattBForde@gmail.com

Thank you for reading.

Also by MB Forde

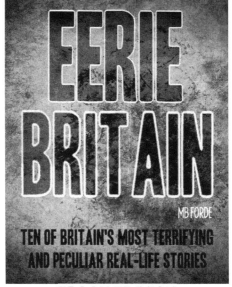

EBOOK EDITION

"Addictive reading."

"The research is excellent, the writing is gripping."

"The top primer to anyone unfamiliar with Britain's scariest legends."

Also by MB Forde

EBOOK EDITION

"A spine-tingling read for all those who wish to curl up in bed with their Kindle...just remember to leave the lights on." — *Phenomenon Magazine*

Also by MB Forde

SNOWS of the NEW YEAR

MB Forde

Snows of the New Year is a gripping, novelette-length vampire ebook.

It is New Year's Eve, 1855. Lord Falin Graeling looks down upon the darkening London skyline from his lofty perch. Sounds of revelry drift up to him on the cold windless air as he awaits the messenger. But assassins appear in the messenger's stead and Falin realises that the dying, fanatical Order of the Knights Venator poses a far more terrible danger than was thought. Together with the seductive and deadly vampiress, Elizabet Athelyn, Falin stalks through the city's shadows in search of a most dangerous enemy.

Also by MB Forde

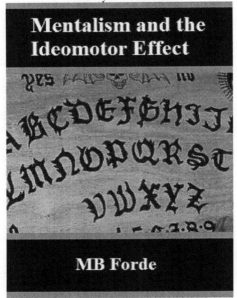

EBOOK EDITION

Even in this science-embracing age, dowsing, Ouija boards and the world of the psychic medium all have their staunch adherents and resolute practitioners. What might come as a surprise to many though, is that a 'true' reading of the mind does indeed seem to exist—and has done for over a century at least. Coincidentally, it also manages to debunk the coat-hanger-based assertions of the dowsing rod and the illusory perils of the Ouija board at the same time. It is called the ideomotor effect.

Part 1: Origins, Real-Life Mind Reading and Dude's Brain Found in his Chest

Part 2: Modern Mentalism and the Real Truth behind Ouija Boards

Part 3: How to Read Minds Yourself

Eerie Britain

Printed in Poland
by Amazon Fulfillment
Poland Sp. z o.o., Wrocław